I0415906

U.S. DEPARTMENT OF LABOR
Employment Standards Administration
Office of Federal Contract Compliance Programs

OFFICE OF FEDERAL CONTRACT COMPLIANCE PROGRAMS

EMPLOYMENT RESOURCE REFERRAL DIRECTORY

U.S. Department of Labor
Employment Standards Administration
 Office of Federal Contract Compliance Programs   EMPLOYMENT RESOURCE REFERRAL DIRECTORY

Employment Resource Referral Directory
Document Creation September 30, 2004
Document Last Revised –September 30, 2004
Cross-Reference Section: *D=Disability; W=Women; M=Minority;*
                              V=Veteran; DV=Disabled Veteran; PA=Public Assistance

DISCLAIMER

The Office of Federal Contract Compliance Programs created this Employment Resource Referral Directory to enhance access to various programs that assist in providing job referral services to veterans, individuals with disabilities, women and minority groups. We recognize that this directory may not be all inclusive of job referral resources for affirmative action recruitment and ask that entities wishing to be considered for addition to this directory contact the OFCCP National Office. The address is:

U.S. Department of Labor
Employment Standards Administration
Office of Federal Contract Compliance Programs
200 Constitution Avenue, NW
Room C-3310
Washington, DC 20210

You may also contact us by sending an e-mail message to: OFCCP-Public@dol.gov; or by sending us a fax. The Fax Telephone Number is (202) 693-1304.

We will make every effort to keep this document current and to correct errors brought to our attention.

The referral directory contains information and hypertext pointers to information created and maintained by other public and private organizations. Please be aware that we do not control or guarantee the accuracy, relevance, timeliness, or completeness of this outside information. Further, the inclusion of pointers to particular items in hypertext is not intended to reflect their importance, nor is it intended to endorse any views expressed or recommends products or services offered by the author of the reference or the organization operating the site on which the reference is maintained.

Employment Resource Referral Directory
Document Creation September 30, 2004
Document Last Revised –September 30, 2004
Cross-Reference Section: *D=Disability; W=Women; M=Minority;*
                                         V=Veteran; DV=Disabled Veteran; PA=Public Assistance

TABLE OF CONTENTS

Employment Resource Referral Directory
Document Creation September 30, 2004
Document Last Revised –September 30, 2004
Cross-Reference Section: *D=Disability; W=Women; M=Minority;*
                    V=Veteran; DV=Disabled Veteran; PA=Public Assistance

Employment Resource Referral Directory
Document Creation September 30, 2004
Document Last Revised –September 30, 2004
Cross-Reference Section: D=Disability; W=Women; M=Minority;
                                    V=Veteran; DV=Disabled Veteran; PA=Public Assistance

Employment Resource Referral Directory
Document Creation September 30, 2004
Document Last Revised –September 30, 2004
Cross-Reference Section: *D=Disability; W=Women; M=Minority;*
                    V=Veteran; DV=Disabled Veteran; PA=Public Assistance

Employment Resource Referral Directory
Document Creation September 30, 2004
Document Last Revised –September 30, 2004
Cross-Reference Section: D=Disability; W=Women; M=Minority;
                              V=Veteran; DV=Disabled Veteran; PA=Public Assistance

Employment Resource Referral Directory
Document Creation September 30, 2004
Document Last Revised –September 30, 2004
Cross-Reference Section: D=Disability; W=Women; M=Minority;
                                   V=Veteran; DV=Disabled Veteran; PA=Public Assistance

Employment Resource Referral Directory
Document Creation September 30, 2004
Document Last Revised –September 30, 2004
Cross-Reference Section: D=Disability; W=Women; M=Minority;
                                     V=Veteran; DV=Disabled Veteran; PA=Public Assistance

Employment Resource Referral Directory
Document Creation September 30, 2004
Document Last Revised –September 30, 2004
Cross-Reference Section: *D=Disability; W=Women; M=Minority;*
                                   V=Veteran; DV=Disabled Veteran; PA=Public Assistance

Employment Resource Referral Directory
Document Creation September 30, 2004
Document Last Revised –September 30, 2004
Cross-Reference Section: D=Disability; W=Women; M=Minority;
                              V=Veteran; DV=Disabled Veteran; PA=Public Assistance

Employment Resource Referral Directory
Document Creation September 30, 2004
Document Last Revised –September 30, 2004
Cross-Reference Section: *D=Disability; W=Women; M=Minority;*
                                         V=Veteran; DV=Disabled Veteran; PA=Public Assistance

Employment Resource Referral Directory
Document Creation September 30, 2004
Document Last Revised –September 30, 2004
Cross-Reference Section: D=Disability; W=Women; M=Minority;
                                      V=Veteran; DV=Disabled Veteran; PA=Public Assistance

Employment Resource Referral Directory
Document Creation September 30, 2004
Document Last Revised –September 30, 2004
Cross-Reference Section: *D=Disability; W=Women; M=Minority;*
                    V=Veteran; DV=Disabled Veteran; PA=Public Assistance

Employment Resource Referral Directory
Document Creation September 30, 2004
Document Last Revised –September 30, 2004
Cross-Reference Section: *D=Disability; W=Women; M=Minority;*
                                   V=Veteran; DV=Disabled Veteran; PA=Public Assistance

Employment Resource Referral Directory
Document Creation September 30, 2004
Document Last Revised –September 30, 2004
Cross-Reference Section: *D=Disability; W=Women; M=Minority;*
                                    V=Veteran; DV=Disabled Veteran; PA=Public Assistance

Employment Resource Referral Directory
Document Creation September 30, 2004
Document Last Revised –September 30, 2004
Cross-Reference Section: D=Disability; W=Women; M=Minority;
                                    V=Veteran; DV=Disabled Veteran; PA=Public Assistance

Employment Resource Referral Directory
Document Creation September 30, 2004
Document Last Revised –September 30, 2004
Cross-Reference Section: *D=Disability; W=Women; M=Minority;*
                              V=Veteran; DV=Disabled Veteran; PA=Public Assistance

Employment Resource Referral Directory
Document Creation September 30, 2004
Document Last Revised –September 30, 2004
Cross-Reference Section: D=Disability; W=Women; M=Minority;
                        V=Veteran; DV=Disabled Veteran; PA=Public Assistance

Employment Resource Referral Directory
Document Creation September 30, 2004
Document Last Revised –September 30, 2004
Cross-Reference Section: *D=Disability; W=Women; M=Minority;*
                                    V=Veteran; DV=Disabled Veteran; PA=Public Assistance

PACIFIC REGION

EMPLOYMENT RESOURCE REFERRAL DIRECTORY

Employment Resource Referral Directory
Document Creation September 30, 2004
Document Last Revised –September 30, 2004
Cross-Reference Section: *D=Disability; W=Women; M=Minority;*
                                  V=Veteran; DV=Disabled Veteran; PA=Public Assistance

PACIFIC REGION

A. *Services Listed by State*

Alaska

90.3 FM KOHNIC Radio Station

810 East 9th Ave
Anchorage, AK 99501
Telephone: (907) 258-8880

Cross-Reference/Focus:PA

Charter College Placement Office

2221 E. Northern Lights Blvd.
Anchorage, AK 99508
Telephone: (907) 277-1000

Cross-Reference/Focus:PA

Employment Training Center

645 G Street, Suite 101
Anchorage, AK 99501
Telephone: (907) 343-4500

Cross-Reference/Focus:PA

First National Bank of Anchorage

425 G Street, Suite 840
Anchorage, AK 99501
Telephone: (907) 265-3069

Cross-Reference/Focus:PA

Job Corps

406 West Fireweed Lane
Anchorage, AK 99503
Telephone: (907) 562-6200

Cross-Reference/Focus:PA

Job Ready Inc.

600 Barrow, Suite 404
Anchorage, AK 99501
Telephone: (907) 258-3498

Cross-Reference/Focus:PA

Job Training Partnership Act

P.O. BOX 196650
Anchorage, AK 99519-6650
Telephone: (907) 343-6560

Cross-Reference/Focus:PA

King Career Center

2650 E. Northern Lights Blvd.
Anchorage, AK 99508
Telephone: (907) 578-9631

Cross-Reference/Focus:PA

Muldoon Community Development Corporation

P.O. BOX 210235
Anchorage, AK 99521-0235

Employment Resource Referral Directory
Document Creation September 30, 2004
Document Last Revised –September 30, 2004
Cross-Reference Section: *D=Disability; W=Women; M=Minority;*
V=Veteran; DV=Disabled Veteran; PA=Public Assistance

Telephone: (907) 250-1680

Cross-Reference/Focus:PA

Northwest Tech

3330 Arctic Blvd., Suite 201
Anchorage, AK 99503
Telephone: (907) 562-6452

Cross-Reference/Focus:PA

Older Persons Action Group

325 E. 3rd Ave., Suite 300
Anchorage, AK 99501
Telephone: (907) 278-1059

Cross-Reference/Focus:PA

Senior Center of Anchorage

1300 E. 19th Ave
Anchorage, AK 99501
Telephone: (907) 258-7823

Cross-Reference/Focus:PA

Work First

3401 Minnesota Drive
Anchorage, AK 99503
Telephone: (907) 258-3122

Cross-Reference/Focus:PA

University of Alaska – Kuskokwim Campus

P.O. BOX 368
Bethel, AK 99559

Telephone: (907) 543-4500

Cross-Reference/Focus:PA

Eagle River Job Service

11723 Old Glenn Highway, #B4
Eagle River, AK 99577
Telephone: (907) 694-6904

Cross-Reference/Focus:PA

EAFB Family Support Group

1890 36th Street
Elmendorf AFB, AK 99506
Telephone: (907) 552-4943

Cross-Reference/Focus:PA

Doyon Corporation

201 1st Ave., Suite 300
Fairbanks, AK 99701
Telephone: (907) 452-4755

Cross-Reference/Focus:PA

Job Assistance Center

Bldg 3723 Neely Road
Ft. Wainwright, AK 99703
Telephone: (907) 353-2096

Cross-Reference/Focus:PA

Sealaska Corporation

One Sealaska Corp., Suite 400
Juneau, AK 99801-1276

Employment Resource Referral Directory
Document Creation September 30, 2004
Document Last Revised –September 30, 2004
Cross-Reference Section: D=Disability; W=Women; M=Minority;
V=Veteran; DV=Disabled Veteran; PA=Public Assistance

Telephone: (907) 586-1823

Cross-Reference/Focus:PA

Career Services Center

3211 Providence Drive
Kodiak, AK 99508
Telephone: (907) 786-4351

Cross-Reference/Focus:PA

Nine Star Enterprises

125 West 5th Ave
Anchorage, AK 99501-2521
Telephone: (907) 279-7827

Cross-Reference/Focus:PA

California

Westside Center for Independent Living, Inc

Mary Ann Jonco, Director
12901 Venice Blvd.
Los Angeles, CA 90066
Telephone: (310) 390-3611
Fax: (310) 390-4906
E-Mail: wcil@wcil.org
Website: www.wcil.org

Cross-Reference: D

Braille Institute

John Silver, Career Service Consultant
Career Services Dept
741 N. Vermont Avenue
Los Angeles, CA 90029

Telephone: (323) 663-1111, Ext. 3134
Fax: (323) 663-0241
E-Mail: jhsilver@brailleinstitute.org
Website: www.brailleinstitute.org

Cross-Reference: D

City of Los Angeles' Department on Disability

Sharon Morris, Executive Director
Ralph Acuna, Information Referral Specialist
333 S. Spring Street, Suite D2
Los Angeles, CA 90013
Telephone: (213) 485-6334
Fax: (213) 485-8052
E-Mail: racuna@mailbox.lacity.org
Website: www.lacity.org/DOD

Cross-Reference: D

Dept of Veterans Affairs - Los Angeles Regional Office

Darlene Theragood, Employment Specialist
11000 Wilshire Blvd., Third Floor
Los Angeles, CA 90024
Telephone: (310) 235-7288/7722
Fax: (310) 235-6247

Cross-Reference: D, DV
E-Mail: vrcdther@rba.va.gov
Website: www.vba.va.gov

State Rehabilitation Program

Sarah Asbury, Rehabilitation Counselor Supervisor
1701 Pacific Avenue, Suite 120
Oxnard, CA 93033
Telephone: (805) 385-2400
Fax: (805) 385-5506
E-Mail: sasbury@dor.ca.gov
Website: www.dor.ca.gov

Employment Resource Referral Directory
Document Creation September 30, 2004
Document Last Revised –September 30, 2004
Cross-Reference Section: *D=Disability; W=Women; M=Minority;*
                    V=Veteran; DV=Disabled Veteran; PA=Public Assistance

---

Cross-Reference: D

Bridges

Susan Addleman, Director
3200 Wilshire Blvd., South Tower
Suite 1207
Los Angeles, CA 90010
Telephone: (213) 381-1220, Ext. 16
Fax: (213) 381-3907
E-Mail: susan.addleman@marriott.com
Website: www.marriottfoundation.org

Cross-Reference: D

Community Rehabilitation Center

Becky Tschirgi, Executive Director
1500 E. Anaheim St.
Long Beach, CA 90813
Telephone: (562) 591-0539
Fax: (562) 599-2872
E-Mail: crimail@cri-lb.org

Cross-Reference: D

Exceptional Children PAR Services

Shirley Bianca, Director of Rehabilitation
8740 Washington Blvd.
Culver City, CA 90232
Telephone: (310) 204-3300
Fax: 845-8001
E-Mail: infoecf@efc.net
Website: www.ecf.net

Cross-Reference: D

Work Training Programs, Inc.

Lisa Padgett, Program Manager
2587 Teller Road

Newbury Park, CA 91320
Telephone: (805) 498-8068, Ext. 113
Fax: (805) 498-1257
E-Mail: lpadgett@wtpinc.org
Website: www.wtpinc.org

Cross-Reference: D, DV, M, W, PA

Chrysalis at New Directions

Brigitte Slayton, Program Manager
11303 Wilshire Blvd.
VA Building 116
Los Angeles, CA 90073
Telephone: (310) 914-4045 Ext. 201
Fax: (310) 914-5495
E-Mail: slayton8235@aol.com
Website: www.New.irectionsinc.org

Cross-Reference: D, DV

Metro North WorkSource Center

Albert Romero, Service Coordinator
342 San Fernando Road
Los Angeles, CA 90031
Telephone: (323) 539-2000 ext 2097
Fax: (323) 539-2029
TDD: (800) 735-2922
E-Mail: aromero@goodwill@socal.org
Website: www.lagoodwill.org

Cross-Reference: D, DV

Assert, Inc.

Elizabeth Adams, Executive Director
445 W. Palmdale Blvd., Suite J
Palmdale, CA 93551
Telephone: (661) 223-5580
Fax: (661) 223-5584
E-Mail: eadams.assert@sbcglobal.net

Employment Resource Referral Directory
Document Creation September 30, 2004
Document Last Revised –September 30, 2004
Cross-Reference Section: D=Disability; W=Women; M=Minority;
   V=Veteran; DV=Disabled Veteran; PA=Public Assistance

Cross-Reference: PA

Foothill Vocational Opportunities

Jim Hall, Executive Director
789 North Fair Oaks Avenue
Pasadena, CA 91103
Telephone: (626) 449-0218
Fax: (626) 449-4802
E-Mail: info@foothill-voc.org

Cross-Reference: D

Los Angeles Unified School District - Huntington Park Community Adult School

Fred Hermosillo, Principal
6020 Miles Avenue
Huntington Park, CA 90255
Telephone: (323) 581-0168
Fax: (323) 581-5515

Los Angeles Unified School District - Abram Friedman Occupational Center - Career Center/Counseling Office

Charlotte Hermosillo, Advisor Counselor
1646 S. Olive Street
Los Angeles, CA 90015
Telephone: (213) 745-2013 ext. 7022
Fax: (213) 749-9380
E-Mail: chermosi@lausd.k12.ca.us
Website: www.lausd.k12.ca.us

Veterans Services - Ventura County

George Compton, County Veteran Service Officer
1701 Pacific Ave., Suite 110
Oxnard, CA 93033
Telephone: (805) 385-6366

Fax: 385-6371
E-Mail: george.compton@mail.co.ventura.ca.us
Website: www.ventura.org/has/index.htm

Cross-Reference: V, DV

Los Angeles Urban League - City of Pomona One Stop Center

Dorothy Durr, Business Service Manager
246 E. Monterey Avenue
Pomona, CA 91767
Telephone: (909) 623-9741
Fax: (626) 793-7396
E-Mail: ddurr@laul.org
Website: www.laul.org

Cross-Reference: D, W, M

Los Angeles Urban League

Rhonda Holbert, Director of Employees Services
3450 Mount Vernon Drive
Los Angeles, CA 90008
Telephone: (323) 299-9660 Ext. 216
Fax: (323) 299-9888
E-Mail: rholbert@laul.org
Website: www.laul.org

Cross-Reference: D, W, M

Career Planning Center, Inc

Terii Richard, Resource Center Counselor
1623 S. La Cienega Blvd.
Los Angeles, CA 90035
Telephone: (310) 273-6644 Ext. 234
Fax: (310) 273-2363
E-Mail: trichard@cpcla.com
Website: www.careerplanningcenter.com.

Cross-Reference: W, M

Employment Resource Referral Directory
Document Creation September 30, 2004
Document Last Revised –September 30, 2004
Cross-Reference Section: *D=Disability; W=Women; M=Minority;*
                          V=Veteran; DV=Disabled Veteran; PA=Public Assistance

Career Planning Center

Andrea Peterson, Resource Manager
13160 Mindanao Way, Suite 240
Marina del Rey, CA 90212
Telephone: (310) 309-6000
Fax: (310) 309-6032
Website: www.careerplanningcenter.com

Cross-Reference: W, M

Center for Employment Training

Amparo Alvarro, Job Developer
761 South C Street
Oxnard, CA 93030
Telephone: (805) 487-9821
Fax: (805) 487-9821
Website: www.cet.2000.org

Cross-Reference: W, M

Mexican American Opportunities Foundation

Irene Milligan, Director of Employment Training Services
972 S. Goodrich Blvd.
City of Commerce, CA 90022
Telephone: (323) 890-1555
Fax: (323) 890-1556
E-Mail: imilligan@maof.org
Website: www.maof.org

Cross-Reference: M

Women in Non-Traditional Employment Roles

Kamla Sullivan, Administrator
P. O. Box 90511
3447 Atlantic Avenue
Long Beach, CA 90807
Telephone: (562) 570-3764
Fax: (562) 570-3791
Website: www.winterbuild@yahoo.com

Cross-Reference: W

Women at Work

Betty Ann Jansen, Executive Director
50 N. Hill Avenue, Suite 300
Pasadena, CA 91106
Telephone: (626) 796-6870
Fax: (626) 793-7396
E-Mail: womenatwork@earthlink.net
Website: www.womenatwork1.org

Cross-Reference: W

Aztlan Truck Driving School

George Ricchecc, Director
8818 Crocker Street
Los Angeles, CA 90003
Telephone: (323) 778-0498
Fax: 778-0984
E-Mail: aztlan2100@webtv.net
Website: www.universities.com/school/A/Aztlan_Truck_
Driving_School

Cross-Reference: W, M

Camino Real Truck Driving School

Alicia Galindo, Director
13674 East Valley Blvd.
La Fuente, CA 91746
Telephone: (626) 968-9135
Fax: (626) 968-9254
Website: www.crschool.com

Cross-Reference: W, M

Imperial Truck Driving School

Joe Henriquez, Director

Employment Resource Referral Directory
Document Creation September 30, 2004
Document Last Revised –September 30, 2004
Cross-Reference Section: D=Disability; W=Women; M=Minority;
                                     V=Veteran; DV=Disabled Veteran; PA=Public Assistance

6101 Wilmington Avenue
Los Angeles, CA 9001-1825
Telephone: (323) 581-7131
Fax: (323) 581-7134
E-Mail: imperialtruckschool@sbcglobal.net
Website: www.imperialtruckdrivingschool.com

Cross-Reference: W, M

Idaho

The Arc, Inc. – Boise

Righ Makovsky
P.O. Box 1061
Boise, Idaho 83701
Telephone: (208) 343-5583

Cross-Reference / Focus: D

The Arc, Inc. – Nampa

Sue Garber
1224 1st Street S
Nampa, Idaho 83651
Telephone: (208) 465-0111

Cross-Reference / Focus: D

Agency for New Americans

Adrian Klemme
1614 W Jefferson Street
Boise, Idaho 83702
Telephone: (208) 338-0033 x35

Cross-Reference / Focus: PA

American Indian Science and Engineering Society

Isabel Bond
U of I; College of Education Room 107
Moscow, Idaho 83844
Telephone: (208) 885-6205

Cross-Reference / Focus: PA

Boise State University - Women's Center/Cultural Center

Debby Woodall
1910 University Drive
Boise, Idaho 83725
Telephone: (208) 426-2407

Cross-Reference / Focus: W

Hispanic Business Association

Alice Witney
10624 W Executive Dr.
Boise, Idaho 83713
Telephone: (208) 322-7033

Cross-Reference / Focus: M

Idaho Migrant Council-Burley

Araceli Mejia
03 E 200 S
Burley, Idaho
Telephone: (208) 678-1171

Cross-Reference / Focus: PA

Idaho Migrant Council-Caldwell

Juan Pablo Cepeda
317 Happy Day Blvd., Suite 250
Caldwell, Idaho 83607
Telephone: (208) 454-8604

Employment Resource Referral Directory
Document Creation September 30, 2004
Document Last Revised –September 30, 2004
Cross-Reference Section: D=Disability; W=Women; M=Minority;
                          V=Veteran; DV=Disabled Veteran; PA=Public Assistance

Cross-Reference / Focus: PA

Idaho Migrant Council-Payette

Juan Pablo Cepeda
540 S 16th Street
Payette, Idaho 83661
Telephone: (208) 642-9304

Cross-Reference / Focus: PA

Idaho Migrant Council-Twin Falls

Andy Rodgriguez (temp)
406 Gardner Avenue
Twin Falls, Idaho 83301
Telephone: (208) 734-3336

Cross-Reference / Focus: PA

Idaho Migrant Council-Blackfoot

Lew Rodriguez
60 Cedar
Blackfoot, Idaho 83221
Telephone: (208) 785-6390

Cross-Reference / Focus: PA

Idaho Migrant Council-Idaho Falls

Lew Rodriguez
637 Park Avenue
Idaho Falls, Idaho 83402
Telephone: (208) 524-0980

Cross-Reference / Focus: PA

KID AM 590 Radio

Domingo Munoz
1655 South Woodruff
Idaho Falls, Idaho 86404
Telephone: (208) 524-9195

Cross-Reference / Focus: PA

Industrial Professional

1119 Ironwood Pkwy
Cour'd Alene, ID 83814
Telephone: (208) 765-2000

Cross-Reference/Focus:PA

Pan Handle Council

11100 Airport Drive
Hayden Lake, ID 83835
Telephone: (208) 772-0584

Cross-Reference/Focus:PA

Oregon

The New Workforce Department

Judy Hassoun/Teresa Bender
4000 Lancaster Dr. NE
Salem, Oregon 97309
Telephone: (503) 399-6547

Cross-Reference / Focus: PA

Adult Learning Skills Program

Brenda Brecke

Employment Resource Referral Directory
Document Creation September 30, 2004
Document Last Revised –September 30, 2004
Cross-Reference Section: D=Disability; W=Women; M=Minority;
                                        V=Veteran; DV=Disabled Veteran; PA=Public Assistance

1988 Newmark
Coos Bay, Oregon 97420
Telephone: (503) 541-888-7121

Cross-Reference / Focus: PA

Centro Latino Americano

Alberto Urquilla
944 W 5th Avenue
Eugene, Oregon 97402
Telephone: (541) 687-2667

Cross-Reference / Focus: M

Changing Directions

Carolyn Esky / Marlene Ream
2600 NW College Way
Bend, Oregon 97701
Telephone: (541) 383-7589

Cross-Reference / Focus: PA

Community Action Organization

Winnie Althizer
1001 SW Baseline
Hillsboro, Oregon 97123
Telephone: (503) 693-3257
E-Mail: Walthizer@caowash.org

Cross-Reference / Focus: PA

Construction Workforce Clearinghouse

Jenny Portis
4106 N Vancouver
Portland, Oregon 97217

Cross-Reference / Focus: PA

Cow Creek Band of Umpqua Tribe of Indians

Martha Young-Foundation Administrator
2371 NE Stephens; Suite 100
Roseburg, Oregon 97470
Telephone: (541) 672-9405

Cross-Reference / Focus: M

Douglas WorkLinks

846 SE Pine St.
Roseburg, Oregon 97470
Telephone: (541) 440-3344

Cross-Reference / Focus: PA

El Programa Hispano

Juan Ocano
451 NW First Street
Gresham, Oregon 97030
Telephone: (503) 669-8350

Cross-Reference / Focus: M

Filipino American Association

Fred Austria
8917 SE Stark
Portland, Oregon 97216
Telephone: (503) 253-7636

Cross-Reference / Focus: M

Goodwill Industries of Oregon

Jim Worley
1943 SE 6th
Portland, Oregon 97214
Telephone: (503) 238-6176

Employment Resource Referral Directory
Document Creation September 30, 2004
Document Last Revised –September 30, 2004
Cross-Reference Section: D=Disability; W=Women; M=Minority;
                                   V=Veteran; DV=Disabled Veteran; PA=Public Assistance

Cross-Reference / Focus: DV

Hispanic Access Center

Lupe McKee-Manager
1533 E Burnside
Portland, Oregon 97217
Telephone: (503) 236-9670

Cross-Reference / Focus: M

Hood River Career Center

Rebecca Bennett
1102 12th Street
Hood River, Oregon 97031
Telephone: (541) 386-6300

Cross-Reference / Focus: PA

Housing Authority of Portland

Jim Trapp
135 SW Ash, 3rd Floor
Portland, Oregon 97204
Telephone: (503) 802-8366

Cross-Reference / Focus: PA

International Refugee Service Program

Debi Houghton / Miriam Ali
10301 NE Glisan
Portland, Oregon 97214
Telephone: (503) 234-1541

Cross-Reference / Focus: W, M, V

Job Corps Placement

Bob Williams
1130 SW Morrison, Suite 525
Springsdale, Oregon
Telephone: (503) 695-2245 ext. 252

Cross-Reference / Focus: W, M, V, DV

Life & Career Options

Jackie Hubka / Betsey Rixford
19600 S Molalla Avenue
Oregon City, Oregon 97045
Telephone: (503) 657-6958 ext. 5161

Cross-Reference / Focus: W, M, V, DV

Lives in Transition

Elaine Heck
1653 Jerome Avenue
Astoria, Oregon 97103
Telephone: (503) 338-2377

Cross-Reference / Focus: W, M, V, DV

Mid-Columbia Council of Governments

Bonnie Myatt
1215 Taylor Street
Hood River, Oregon 97031
Telephone: (541) 389-6300

Cross-Reference / Focus: W, M, V, DV

Mid-Columbia Council of Governments

Darlene Stevens
1113 Kelly Avenue
Dalles, Oregon 97058

Employment Resource Referral Directory
Document Creation September 30, 2004
Document Last Revised –September 30, 2004
Cross-Reference Section: D=Disability; W=Women; M=Minority;
                               V=Veteran; DV=Disabled Veteran; PA=Public Assistance

Telephone: (541) 298-4101

Cross-Reference / Focus: PA

Moving On

Serena St. Clair
3345 Redwood Highway
Grants Pass, Oregon 97527

Cross-Reference / Focus: PA

Mt. Hood Community College Workforce Connections

Tanya Mead / Betsy Pfannenstiel
4510 NE 102nd
Portland, Oregon 97220
Telephone: (503) 252-0758

Cross-Reference / Focus: DV, D, V

Mt. Hood Community College – Steps to Success East

Guy Crawford / Steve Vieria
14030 NE Sacramento Street
Portland, Oregon 97230
Telephone: (503) 256-0431

Cross-Reference / Focus: DV, D, V

NE One-Stop Career Center

3034 NE Martin Luther King Blvd.
Portland, Oregon 97212
Telephone: (503) 241-4644

Cross-Reference / Focus: PA

New Directions

Christine Paull
Portland Community College - Rock Creek
P.O. Box 19000
Portland Oregon 97280
Telephone: (503) 614-7448

Cross-Reference / Focus: PA

ODOT

Vernell West
On-The-Job Training Support Service Provider
431 NE Jarrett
Portland, Oregon 97211
Telephone: (503) 493-6027
E-Mail: Vwservices@aol.com

Cross-Reference / Focus: PA

Oregon Institute of Technology Career Services

Jan Todd
3201 Campus Drive
Klamath Falls, Oregon 97601
Telephone: (541) 885-1020

Cross-Reference / Focus: PA

Oregon Council for Hispanic Advancement

Greg Acuna
108 NW 9th, Suite 108
Portland, Oregon 97209
Telephone: (503) 228-4131 / (503) 241-9965

Cross-Reference: M

Employment Resource Referral Directory
Document Creation September 30, 2004
Document Last Revised –September 30, 2004
Cross-Reference Section: D=Disability; W=Women; M=Minority;
                              V=Veteran; DV=Disabled Veteran; PA=Public Assistance

Oregon Human Development Corporation Youth Center

Joe Estrada
233 SE Washington
Hillsboro, Oregon 97123
Telephone: (503) 640-6349

Cross-Reference / Focus: PA

Oregon Tradeswomen Network

Connie Ashbrook
1714 NE Alberta
Portland, Oregon 97211
Telephone: (503) 335-8200

Cross-Reference / Focus: W

Portland Community College Skills Center

Ed Joseph / James Bowles
739 NE Killingsworth
Portland, Oregon 97217
Telephone: (503) 978-5343

Cross-Reference / Focus: PA

PCC Steps to Success

Leah Dumas / Miriam Freedman
North & Metro Center
4317 NE Emerson
Portland, Oregon 97218
Telephone: (503) 943-2000

Cross-Reference / Focus: PA

Portland Youth Builders

Jim Walters / Duke Moten

7332 N Smith
Portland, Oregon 97217
Telephone: (503) 286-9350

Cross-Reference / Focus: PA

SE Works One Stop

Susan Eastman
6927 SE Foster Rd.
Portland, Oregon 97206
Telephone: (503) 772-2301

Cross-Reference / Focus: PA

The Job Council – Grants Pass

Linda Draper
1545 Harbeck Rd.
Grants Pass, Oregon 97527
Telephone: (541) 476-1187 x303

Cross-Reference / Focus: PA

The Job Council – Medford

Pam Farquhar
673 Market Street
Medford, Oregon 97504
Telephone: (541) 776-5100 x2170

Cross-Reference / Focus: PA

Transitions

Cynthia Dettman / Clondy Navarro
26000 SE Stark Street
Gresham, Oregon 97030
Telephone: (503) 491-7687

Cross-Reference / Focus: PA

Employment Resource Referral Directory
Document Creation September 30, 2004
Document Last Revised –September 30, 2004
Cross-Reference Section: *D=Disability; W=Women; M=Minority;*
V=Veteran; DV=Disabled Veteran; PA=Public Assistance

Transitions to Success

Kate Barry
4000 E 30th Avenue
Eugene, Oregon 97405
Telephone: (541) 463-5264

Cross-Reference / Focus: PA

Turning Point Transitions Program

Dawn McNannay
6500 Pacific Boulevard SW
Albany, Oregon 97321
Telephone: (541) 917-4875

Cross-Reference / Focus: PA

Ucan Transitions Programs – Confidence Clinic

Anna William / Linda Brown
1140 College Rd.
Roseburg, Oregon 97470
Telephone: (541) 672-5392

Cross-Reference / Focus: PA

Umpqua Training & Employment

760 NW Hill Ave.
Roseburg, Oregon 97470
Telephone: (541) 672-7761

Cross-Reference / Focus: PA

Wings

Joanne Easterly
650 College Blvd.
Ontario, Oregon 97914
Telephone: (541) 881-8822 ext.285

Cross-Reference / Focus: P

Washington

Grays Harbor College Counseling Center

1620 Edward P. Smith Drive
Aberdeen, WA 98520
Telephone: (360) 532-9020

Cross-Reference/Focus:PA

Green River Community College

12401 SE 320th St.
Auburn, WA 98002
Telephone: (206) 833-9111

Cross-Reference/Focus:PA

Bellevue Community College

3000 Landerholm Circle SE
Bellevue, WA 98007
Telephone: (425) 564-2215

Cross-Reference/Focus:PA

Whatcom Community Career Center

237 W. Kellog Road
Bellingham, WA 98226
Telephone: (360) 676-2170

Cross-Reference/Focus:PA

Bremerton JSC

Employment Resource Referral Directory
Document Creation September 30, 2004
Document Last Revised –September 30, 2004
Cross-Reference Section: *D=Disability; W=Women; M=Minority;*
     V=Veteran; DV=Disabled Veteran; PA=Public Assistance

4980 Auto Center Way
P.O. BOX 519
Bremerton, WA 98206
Telelphone: (800) 318-6022

Cross-Reference/Focus:PA

Kitsap Community Action Program

1200 Elizabeth Ave
Bremerton, WA 98312
Telephone: (360) 377-0053

Cross-Reference/Focus:PA

Centralia College

600 West Locust
Centralia, WA 98225
Telephone: (360) 736-9391

Cross-Reference/Focus:PA

Walla Walla College

204 South College Ave
College Place, WA 99324
Telephone: (509) 527-2357

Cross-Reference/Focus:PA

Everett Community College

2000 Tower Street
Everett, WA 98201
Telephone: (425) 388-9549

Cross-Reference/Focus:PA

Everett JSC

840 Broadway North
Everett, WA 98206
Telephone: (425) 339-4921

Cross-Reference/Focus:PA

Everett Public Library

2702 Hoyt Ave
Everett, WA 98201
Telephone: (425) 257-8012

Cross-Reference/Focus:PA

South King County Multiservice Center

1200 South 336th St.
Federal Way, WA 98003
Telephone: (253) 838-6810

Cross-Reference/Focus:PA

Lake Washington Technical College

11605 132nd Ave N.E
Kirkland, WA 98034
Telephone: (425) 739-8131

Cross-Reference/Focus:PA

St. Martins College

5300 Pacific Ave
Lacey, WA 98503
Telephone: (206) 291-4700

Cross-Reference/Focus:PA

Employment Resource Referral Directory
Document Creation September 30, 2004
Document Last Revised –September 30, 2004
Cross-Reference Section: *D=Disability; W=Women; M=Minority;*
V=Veteran; DV=Disabled Veteran; PA=Public Assistance

Clover Park Technical College

4500 Steilacoom Blvd.
Lakewood, WA 98499
Telephone: (253) 589-5541

Cross-Reference/Focus:PA

Lower Columbia College

P.O. BOX 3010
Longview, WA 98632
Telephone: (360) 577-5449

Cross-Reference/Focus:PA

Edmonds Community College

20000 68th Ave West
Lynnwood, WA 98036
Telephone: (425) 640-1443

Cross-Reference/Focus:PA

Highline Community College Job Referral

2400 South 24th M/S 610
Midway, WA 98031
Telephone: (206) 878-3710

Cross-Reference/Focus:PA

Mt. Vernon JSC

301 Valley Mall Way Suite 110
Mt. Vernon, WA 98273
Telephone: (360) 675-3403

Northwest Washington Private Industry Council

2021 E. College Way Suite 210
Mt. Vernon, WA 98273
Telephone: (360) 671-1660

Cross-Reference/Focus:PA

Port Angeles JSC

1601 East Front Street
Port Angeles, WA 98362
Telephone: (360) 457-9407

Cross-Reference/Focus:PA

LDS Employment General Services

220 South 3rd Place
Renton, WA 98055
Telephone: (206) 682-3363

Cross-Reference/Focus:PA

Puget Sound OIC

801 S.W. 16th Street, Suite 104
Renton, WA 98055
Telephone: (425) 227-5114

Cross-Reference/Focus:PA

Renton Technical College

3000 NE 4th Street
Renton, WA 98056
Telephone: (425) 235-5840

Cross-Reference/Focus:PA

Center for Career Alternatives

Employment Resource Referral Directory
Document Creation September 30, 2004
Document Last Revised –September 30, 2004
Cross-Reference Section: *D=Disability; W=Women; M=Minority;*
V=Veteran; DV=Disabled Veteran; PA=Public Assistance

901 Rainier Ave South
Seattle, WA 98144
Telephone: (206) 322-9080

Cross-Reference/Focus:PA

Centerpoint Institute for Life and Career Removal

1326 5th Ave, Suite 658
Seattle, WA 98101
Telephone: (206) 622-8070

Cross-Reference/Focus:PA

Church Council of Greater Seattle

4759 15th Ave NE
Seattle, WA 98105
Telephone: (206) 525-1213

Cross-Reference/Focus:PA

City Of Seattle Job Hotline

710 2nd Ave
Seattle, WA 98104
Telephone: (206) 684-7999

Cross-Reference/Focus:PA

Delridge OnRamp Career and Computer Access Center

4501 Delridge Way SW
Seattle, WA 98106
Telephone: (206) 933-8629

Cross-Reference/Focus:PA

Downtown Human Services Council

115 Prefontaine Place South
Seattle, WA 98104
Telephone: (206) 461-3865

Cross-Reference/Focus:PA

Employment Opportunities Center

12550 Aurora Ave North
Seattle, WA 98133
Telephone: (206) 440-2562

Cross-Reference/Focus:PA

Farestart

1902 2nd Ave South
Seattle, WA 98101
Telephone: (206) 443-1233

Cross-Reference/Focus:PA

Fremont Public Association

1501 North 45th Street
Seattle, WA 98103
Telephone: (206) 461-3200

Cross-Reference/Focus:PA

Greater Seattle Chamber of Commerce

1301 5th Ave, Suite 2400
Seattle, WA 98101
Telephone: (206) 389-7310

Cross-Reference/Focus:PA

Employment Resource Referral Directory
Document Creation September 30, 2004
Document Last Revised –September 30, 2004
Cross-Reference Section: D=Disability; W=Women; M=Minority;
      V=Veteran; DV=Disabled Veteran; PA=Public Assistance

International Examiner

622 S. Washington Street
Seattle, WA 98104
Telephone: (206) 624-3925

Jewish Family Services

1601 16th Ave
Seattle, WA 98122
Telephone: (206) 461-3240

Cross-Reference/Focus:PA

Job Corps, Department of Labor

810 3rd Ave
Seattle, WA 98104
Telephone: (206) 622-6593

Cross-Reference/Focus:PA

King 5 Television

333 Dexter Ave North
Seattle, WA 98109
Telephone: (206) 448-5555

Cross-Reference/Focus:PA

KTZZ-Channel 21

945 Dexter Ave North
Seattle, WA 98109
Telephone: (206) 282-2202

Cross-Reference/Focus:PA

Metrocenter YMCA

909 4th Ave 6th Floor
Seattle, WA 98104
Telephone: (206) 382-5013

Cross-Reference/Focus:PA

Millionaire Club

2515 Western Ave
Seattle, WA 98121
Telephone: (206) 728-JOBS

Cross-Reference/Focus:PA

North American Post

622-1/2 South Jackson
P.O. BOX 3171
Seattle, WA 98104
Telephone: (206) 623-0100

Cross-Reference/Focus:PA

North Seattle Community College

9600 College Way North
Seattle, WA 98103
Telephone: (206) 527-3685

Cross-Reference/Focus:PA

Pacific Associates

2200 6th Ave, Suite 260
Seattle, WA 98121
Telephone: (206) 728-8826

Cross-Reference/Focus:PA

Employment Resource Referral Directory
Document Creation September 30, 2004
Document Last Revised –September 30, 2004
Cross-Reference Section: D=Disability; W=Women; M=Minority;
                                   V=Veteran; DV=Disabled Veteran; PA=Public Assistance

U.S. Department of Labor
Employment Standards Administration
Office of Federal Contract Compliance Programs

EMPLOYMENT RESOURCE REFERRAL DIRECTORY

Park Lake Neighborhood House

10041 6th Ave S.W
Seattle, WA 98146
Telephone: (206) 767-7124

Cross-Reference/Focus:PA

Pike Market Senior Employment Program

1931 1st Ave
Seattle, WA 98101
Telephone: (206) 728-2773

Cross-Reference/Focus:PA

Rainier JSC

2531 Rainier Ave South
P.O. BOX 22510
Seattle, WA 98122
Telephone: (206) 721-6000

Cross-Reference/Focus:PA

Rainier Vista Job Resource Center

4414 Tamarack Drive South
Seattle, WA 98108
Telephone: (206) 760-9513

Cross-Reference/Focus:PA

Salvation Army

P.O. BOX 46333
Seattle, WA 98146
Telephone: (206) 767-3150

Cross-Reference/Focus:PA

Seattle Central Community College

1701 Broadway
Seattle, WA 98122
Telephone: (206) 344-4383

Cross-Reference/Focus:PA

Seattle Conservation Corps

7400 Sand Point Way N.E
Seattle, WA 98115
Telephone: (206) 684-0190

Cross-Reference/Focus:PA

Seattle Housing Authority

6564 32nd S.W
Seattle, WA 98126
Telephone: (206) 615-3300

Cross-Reference/Focus:PA

Seattle Post Intelligence

P.O. BOX 1909
Seattle, WA 98121
Telephone: (206) 448-8000

Seattle Public Library

1000 4th Ave
Seattle, WA 98104
Telephone: (206) 386-4620

Seattle Vocational Institute

2120 South Jackson Street
Seattle, WA 98144

Employment Resource Referral Directory
Document Creation September 30, 2004
Document Last Revised –September 30, 2004
Cross-Reference Section: *D=Disability; W=Women; M=Minority;*
                    V=Veteran; DV=Disabled Veteran; PA=Public Assistance

Telephone: (206) 587-4950

Cross-Reference/Focus:PA

Shoreline Community College

161091 Greenwood Ave N.
Seattle, WA 98133
Telephone: (206) 546-7844

Cross-Reference/Focus:PA

Sound Opportunities

P.O. BOX 16722
Seattle, WA 98116
Telephone: (206) 933-6556

Cross-Reference/Focus:PA

South Seattle Community College

6000 16th Ave S.W
Seattle, WA 98106
Telephone: (206) 764-5304

Cross-Reference/Focus:PA

Student Conservation Association

1265 South Main Street, Suite 210
Seattle, WA 98144
Telephone: (206) 324-4649

Cross-Reference/Focus:PA

Tacoma True Citizen

1206 South Bldg.
Seattle, WA 98405

Telephone: (206) 627-1103

Cross-Reference/Focus:PA

The Fact Newspaper

2765 East Cherry
Seattle, WA 98122
Telephone: (206) 324-0552

Cross-Reference/Focus:PA

The Medium

2600 South Jackson St.
Seattle, WA 98122
Telephone: (206) 323-0070

Cross-Reference/Focus:PA

University of Washington

301 Loew Hall, Main Campus Box 352190
Seattle, WA 98195
Telephone: (206) 543-0535

Cross-Reference/Focus:PA

Washington State Employment Security Program

2106 2nd Ave
Seattle, WA 98101
Telephone: (206) 721-5990

Washington Works

616 1st Ave, 5th Floor
Seattle, WA 98104
Telephone: (206) 343-9731

Employment Resource Referral Directory
Document Creation September 30, 2004
Document Last Revised –September 30, 2004
Cross-Reference Section: *D=Disability; W=Women; M=Minority;*
                          V=Veteran; DV=Disabled Veteran; PA=Public Assistance

Cross-Reference/Focus:PA

Cross-Reference/Focus:PA

Worker Center, AFL-CIO

2800 1st Ave, Suite 250
Seattle, WA 98121
Telephone: (206) 461-3220

Cross-Reference/Focus:PA

Workfirst Program

2106 2nd Ave
Seattle, WA 98121
Telephone: (206) 959-3325

Cross-Reference/Focus:PA

YMCA

909 4th Ave
Seattle, WA 98104
Telephone: (206) 382-5003

Cross-Reference/Focus:PA

Employment Counseling Center

SE 70th Squaxin Lane
Shelton, WA 98584
Telephone: (360) 426-9781

Cross-Reference/Focus:PA

Center for Human Services

17018 15th Ave NE
Shoreline, WA 98155
Telephone: (206) 362-7282

Job Resource Center

Great Western Bldg., Suite 507905, West Riverside
Spokane, WA 99201
Telephone: (509) 747-3071

Cross-Reference/Focus:PA

Spokane Community College

1810 North Green Street
Spokane, WA 99207
Telephone: (509) 533-7000

Cross-Reference/Focus:PA

Bates Technical College

1101 South Yakima Ave
Tacoma, WA 98405
Telephone: (253) 596-1526

Cross-Reference/Focus:PA

Employment and Training

4505 Pacific HWY East
Tacoma, WA 98424
Telephone: (253) 476-6800

Cross-Reference/Focus:PA

North Dispatch

1108 South 11th Street
Tacoma, WA 98405
Telephone: (253) 272-7587

Employment Resource Referral Directory
Document Creation September 30, 2004
Document Last Revised –September 30, 2004
Cross-Reference Section: *D=Disability; W=Women; M=Minority;*
                              V=Veteran; DV=Disabled Veteran; PA=Public Assistance

Cross-Reference/Focus:PA

Cross-Reference/Focus: PA

Pierce College Career Placement

9401 Farwest Drive SW
Tacoma, WA 98498
Telephone: (253) 964-6705

Cross-Reference/Focus:PA

Vancouver JSC

5411 E. Mail Plane, Suite B
Vancouver, WA 98661
Telephone: (360) 735-4961

Cross-Reference/Focus:PA

Tacoma Community College

6501 S. 19th St. Bldg #12
Tacoma, WA 98465
Telephone: (253) 566-5000

Cross-Reference/Focus:PA

Vashon Youth and Family Services

20200 Vashon Hwy. S.W
Vashon, WA 98070
Telephone: (206) 463-5511

Cross-Reference/Focus:PA

Tacoma Community House

1311 S. M Street
Tacoma, WA 98405
Telephone: (253) 383-3951

Cross-Reference/Focus:PA

Wenatchee Valley College

1300 5th Street
Wenatchee, WA 98801
Telephone: (509) 665-2600

Cross-Reference/Focus:PA

Tacoma News Tribune

P.O. BOX 11000
Tacoma, WA 98411
Telephone: (253) 597-8686

Cross-Reference/Focus:PA

Community Trades and Careers

811 Madison
Everett, WA 90821
Telephone: (425) 353-7521

Cross-Reference/Focus:PA

Tacoma-Pierce Co. Private Industry Council

733 Market Street Rm. 21
Tacoma, WA 98402
Telephone: (253) 591-5450

Nelson & Associates

Mary-Jane Richardson
1111 Main Street, Suite 710
Vancouver, Washington 97214
Telephone: (360) 750-5521

Employment Resource Referral Directory
Document Creation September 30, 2004
Document Last Revised –September 30, 2004
Cross-Reference Section: *D=Disability; W=Women; M=Minority;*
                              V=Veteran; DV=Disabled Veteran; PA=Public Assistance

Cross-Reference / Focus: D

B. Women's Services Listed by State

California

Cypress Mandela – Women in Skilled Trades

Arthur Shanks, Employment Specialist
Jeri Robinson, Executive Director
2229 Poplar Street
Oakland, CA 94607
Telephone: (510) 208-7355
Fax: (510) 835-3726
E-Mail: artshanks@yahoo.com

Cross-Reference / Focus: W

Trades Women, Inc.

Beth Youhn, Executive Director
2485 W. 14th Street
Oakland, CA 94607
Telephone: (510) 891-8778
E-Mail: eyouhn@aol.com

Cross-Reference / Focus: W

Women's Employment Resources Corporation

3362 Adeline Street
Berkeley, CA 94703
Telephone: (510) 652-5484
Fax: (510) 652-4184
E-Mail: werc@lmi.net

Cross-Reference / Focus: W

Women's Employment Resources Corporation

3356 Adeline Street
Berkeley, CA 94703
Telephone: (510) 652-5484

Cross-Reference None   Focus: Females

Computer Training Consultants

144 San Tomas Aquino Road
Campbell, CA 95008
Contact: Kevin Easton, Vice President
Telephone: (408) 871-6636

Cross-Reference: M

Micro-Polytech Institute

1108 Walsh Avenue
Santa Clara, CA 95050
Contact: Alex Le, Director of Training
Telephone: (408) 492-9048

Cross-Reference: M

Institute for Business & Technology, Inc.

2550 Scott Boulevard
Santa Clara, CA 95050
Contact: Anne Batch Dougherty, Director of Placement
Telephone: (408) 727-1060, ext. 225

Central County Occupational Programs - Metropolitan Eduation District

760 Hillsdale Avenue
San Jose, CA 95136
Contact: Shirley Philipson, Career Center Manager

Employment Resource Referral Directory
Document Creation September 30, 2004
Document Last Revised –September 30, 2004
Cross-Reference Section: D=Disability; W=Women; M=Minority;
                    V=Veteran; DV=Disabled Veteran; PA=Public Assistance

Telephone: (408) 723-6416

Cross-Reference: M

Center for Training and Careers, Incorporated

1600 Las Plumas
San Jose, CA 95133
Contact: Job Developer
Fax: 408-251-3146
Telephone: (408) 251-3165
Website: www.ctcsj.org

Cross-Reference: M

One-Stop Career Center (EDD)

2450 South Bascom Avenue
Campbell, CA 95008
Contact: Pam Kenney or Nancy Kwan, Employment
Representatives
Telephone: (408) 369-3606
Telephone: (408) 369-3680

Cross-Reference: M

Cypress-Mandela Training Center - Women in Skilled Trades

2229 Poplar Street
Oakland, CA 94607
Contact: Arthur Shanks, Project Manager
Telephone: (510) 208-7350

National Association of Women in Construction (NAWIC) - Santa Clara County Chapter

18900 Stevens Creek Blovd., Suite 200
Cupertino, CA 95014
Contact: Danijela Mosunic, Outreach Coordinator

Job Corps Center

3485 East Hills Drive
San Jose, CA 95127
Contact: Richard Martinez
Telephone: (408) 254-5627

Math, Engineering, Science Achievement (MESA) - San Jose State University Program

One Washington Square
San Jose, CA 95192-0080
Contact: Horacio Alfaro, Director
Telephone: (408) 924-3830

Cross-Reference: M

Arbor Career Center

344 Salinas Street, Suite 202
Telephone: (831) 751-6002
Contact: Manuela Valdez and Brenda Sorrenson,
Employment Specialists

Cross-Reference: M

Arbor of Santa Cruz County

18 West Beach Street
Watsonville, CA 95076
Contact: Theresa Wright, Director
Telephone: (831) 763-8723

City of Long Beach, Career Transition Center

Lawrence Eberhart, Program Liaison
3447 Atlantic Avenue
Long Beach, CA 90807
Telephone: (562) 570-3654
E-Mail: buhlo@earthlink.net
Website: www.ci.long-beach.ca.us/cd/lbsda

Employment Resource Referral Directory
Document Creation September 30, 2004
Document Last Revised –September 30, 2004
Cross-Reference Section: *D=Disability; W=Women; M=Minority;*
                    V=Veteran; DV=Disabled Veteran; PA=Public Assistance

Cross-Reference / Focus: W, M

Women in Non-Traditional Employment Roles (WINTER)

Becky Lane, Employment Specialist
Lynn Shaw, CEO
Po Box 90511
Long Beach, CA 90809
Telephone: (562) 570-3764
Fax: (562) 430-9181

Cross-Reference / Focus: W

Center for Women and Men (CWM) - University of California, Irvine

Christine Fredericks, Director
100 Gateway Commons
University of California, Irvine
Irvine, CA 92697-5251
Telephone: (949) 824-6000
Fax:(949) 824-3412
E-Mail: cwm@uci.edu
Website: www.cwm.uci.edu

Cross-Reference / Focus: W

Hawaii

Hawaii - Island of Oahu

Alu Like, Inc

Winona Whitman, Director of Employment/Training
458 Keawe St.
Honolulu, HI 96813
Telephone: (808) 535-6750
Fax: (808) 524-3744

Website: www.alulike.org

Cross-Reference/Focus: W, M

Associated Builders & Contractors, Inc. (ABC)

Dana Vennen, Director of Education/Training
207 Puuhale Road, Suite A
Honolulu, HI 96819
Telephone: (808) 845-4887
Fax: (808) 847-7876
Website: www.abc.org/Hawai'i

Cross-Reference/Focus: W, M

Catholic Charities Community & Immigrant Services

Dana Vennen, Director of Education/Training
712 N. School Street
Honolulu, HI 96817
Telephone: (808) 528-5233
Fax: (808) 531-1970

Cross-Reference/Focus: W, M

Department of Labor & Industrial Relations - Workforce Development Division (Honolulu Office)

Suzanne Okazaki, Veterans Program Specialist
830 Punchbowl Street #329
Honolulu, HI 96813
Telephone: (808) 586-8881
Fax: (808) 586-8822
Website: www.dlir.state.hi.us\wdd

Cross-Reference/Focus: W, M, V, D, DV

Goodwill Industries of Hawaii, Inc

Employment Resource Referral Directory
Document Creation September 30, 2004
Document Last Revised –September 30, 2004
Cross-Reference Section: *D=Disability; W=Women; M=Minority;*
                              V=Veteran; DV=Disabled Veteran; PA=Public Assistance

Mr. Dan Buron, Vice President of Human Services
2610 Kilihau Street
Honolulu, HI 96819
Telephone: (808) 836-0313
Fax: (808) 836-2579
E-Mail: dburon@higoodwill.org
Website: www.higoodwill.org

Cross-Reference/Focus: D, M, W, PA

Hawaii Hispanic Chamber of Commerce

Susana Ho, President
P.O. Box 235263
Honolulu, HI 96823
Telephone: (808) 545-4344
Fax: (808) 550-8416

Cross-Reference/Focus: W, M

Hawaii Job Corp.

Lauree Nakata, Employment Transition Coordinator
49 S. Hotel St.
Empire Bldg. #205
Honolulu, HI 96813
Telephone: (808) 545-4344
Fax: (808) 550-8416

Cross-Reference/Focus: W, M

Hispanic Center of Hawaii

Nancy Ortiz, Executive Director
2044 S. Beretania St., Suite 2
Honolulu, HI 96826
Telephone: (808) 941-5216
Fax: (808) 941-1594
Website:
www.hometown.aol.com/latinladydjmv/centrohispano.html

Cross-Reference/Focus: W, M, D, V, DV

Honolulu Community College - Job Placement Office

Lorrie Cahill, Coordinator
720 N. King St.
Honolulu, HI 96817
Telephone: (808) 845-9207
Fax: (808) 847-9829
E-Mail: ulcahill@hcc.Hawai'i.ed
Website: www.hcc.Hawai'i.edu

Cross-Reference/Focus: W, M

Insights to Success, Inc

Ms. Mary Lou Clizbe, Executive Director
Ms. Myra L. Hager, Co-Executive Director
1154 Fort Street Mall, Suite 200
Honolulu, HI 96813
Telephone: (808) 532-8322
Toll free: (877) 532-8322
Fax: (808) 532-8324
E-Mail: its@alliedcom.net

Cross-Reference/Focus: D, M, W, V, DV, PA

JOINT EMPLOYMENT MANAGEMENT SYSTEM (JEMS)

Rita May, Director
Commander Navy Region Hawaii
1025 Quincy Ave., Suite 100
Pearl Harbor, HI 96860-4512
Telephone: (808) 473-0190
Fax: (808) 473-1402
Website: www.jemsHawai'i.com

Cross-Reference/Focus: W, M, V, DV

Leeward Community College - Office of Continuing Education and Training

Employment Resource Referral Directory
Document Creation September 30, 2004
Document Last Revised –September 30, 2004
Cross-Reference Section: *D=Disability; W=Women; M=Minority;*
                              V=Veteran; DV=Disabled Veteran; PA=Public Assistance

Randall Francisco, Director
96-045 Ala Ike St.
Pearl City, HI 96782
Telephone: (808) 455-0477
Fax: (808) 453-6730
Website: www.lcc.Hawai'i.edu/ocet

Cross-Reference/Focus: W, M

National Association of Women in Construction

June Keaton, Past President
94-561 Kuaie Street
Mililani, HI 96789
Telephone: (808) 625-0441 or 833-4401
Fax: (808) 625-6604

Cross-Reference/Focus: W, M

Pacific Gateway Center (formerly The Immigrant Center)

Dr. Tin Myaing Thein, Executive Director
720 N. King St.
Honolulu, HI 96817
Telephone: (808) 845-3918
Fax: (808) 842-1962
Website: www.pacificgateway.org

Cross-Reference/Focus: W, M

Samoan Service Providers Association (SSPA)

William Emmsley, Executive Director
2153 N. King Street #108
Honolulu, HI 96819
Telephone: (808) 842-0218
Fax: (808) 845-6539
E-Mail: sspa@sspa-hi.com
Website: www.samoanserviceproviders.com

Cross-Reference/Focus: W, M, V

YWCA of Oahu

Sharon Gergurson-Quick, V.P. Managing Director
Human Resource Department
1040 Richards Street
Honolulu, HI 96813
Telephone: (808) 538-7061
Fax: (808) 521-8416
Website: www.ywcaoahu.org

Cross-Reference/Focus: W, M

Hawaii - Island of Kauai

Alu Like, Inc.

Remi Meints, Employment Training Coordinator
3100 Kuhio Hwy. C-6, C-7
Lihue, HI 96766
Telephone: (808) 245-8545
Fax: (808) 245-1720
Website: www.alulike.org

Cross-Reference/Focus: W, M,

Department of Labor & Industrial Relations - Workforce Development Division (Job Bank)

Tracy Hirano, Branch Manager
3100 Kuhio Hwy. Ste C-9
Lihue, HI 96766
Telephone: (808) 274-3056
Fax: (808) 274-3059
Website: www.dlir.state.hi.us/wdd/lihue/

Cross-Reference/Focus: D, W, M, V

Kauai Community College

Nia Acob, Cooperative Education Coordinator
31-901 Kaumualii Hwy.

Employment Resource Referral Directory
Document Creation September 30, 2004
Document Last Revised –September 30, 2004
Cross-Reference Section: D=Disability; W=Women; M=Minority;
                                    V=Veteran; DV=Disabled Veteran; PA=Public Assistance

Lihue, HI 96766
Telephone: (808) 245-8328
Fax: (808) 245-8232

Cross-Reference/Focus: W, M

Kauai Economic Opportunity, Inc

Mabel Fujiuchi, Chief Executive Officer
P.O. Box 1027 (2804 Wehe Rd.)
Lihue, HI 96766
Telephone: (808) 245-4077
Fax: (808) 245-7476

Cross-Reference/Focus: W, M

Hawaii - Island of Maui

Alu Like, Inc.

Ms. Marlene Burgess, Employment Training Coordinator
1977 Kaohu Street
Wailuku, Maui, HI 96793
Telephone: (808) 249-9774
Fax: (808) 244-7880
E-Mail: mburgess@alulike.org
Website: www.alulike.org

Cross-Reference/Focus: W, M

Department of Labor and Industrial Relations - Workforce Development Division, Worksource Maui

Mr. Kevin Kimizuka, Acting Maui County Branch Manager
2064 Wells Street, #108
Wailuku, Maui, HI 96793
Telephone: (808) 984-2091
Fax: (808) 984-2090
Website: http://dlir.state.hi.us/wdd/

Cross-Reference/Focus: D, M, W, V, DV, PA

Maui Community College - Cooperative Education and Job Placement Services

Mr. Barry Takahashi, Job Placement and Retention Coordinator
310 Kaahumanu Avenue
Kahului, Maui, HI 96732
Telephone: (808) 984-3353
Fax: (808) 244-3228
E-Mail: uellenh@Hawai'i.ed
Website: http://mauicc.Hawai'i.edu\unit\coop\index.htm

Cross-Reference/Focus: M, W

Maui Economic Opportunity, Inc

Ms. Loretta Pacubas, Community Services Director
99 Mahalani Street
Wailuku, Maui, HI 96793
Telephone: (808) 249-2970
Fax: (808) 249-2971
E-Mail: loretta.pacubas@meoinc.org
Website: www.meo.org

Cross-Reference/Focus: M, W, PA

Hawaii - Island of Molokai

Alu Like Inc. - Molokai Island Center

Ms. Ruth Poaipuni, Employment Training Manager
P. O. Box 1859
Kaunakakai, Molokai, HI 96748
Telephone: (808) 553-5393
Fax: (808) 553-9998
E-Mail: rpoaipuni@alulike.org
Website: www.alulike.org

Cross-Reference/Focus: M, W, V, PA

Employment Resource Referral Directory
Document Creation September 30, 2004
Document Last Revised –September 30, 2004
Cross-Reference Section: D=Disability; W=Women; M=Minority;
                                V=Veteran; DV=Disabled Veteran; PA=Public Assistance

Hawaii - Island of Hawaii

Department of Labor & Industrial Relations - Workforce Development Division (Job Bank)

Lori Sasaki, Kona Office Manager
74-5565 Luhia St., C-4
Kailua-Kona, HI 96740
Telephone: (808) 327-4770
Fax: (808) 327-4774
Website: www.dlir.state.hi.us/wdd/

Cross-Reference/Focus: D, W, M, V

Department of Labor & Industrial Relations - Workforce Development Division

Charlie Kunz, Hilo Office Manager
180 Kinoole St., Suite 205
Hilo, HI 96720
Telephone: (808) 974-4126
Fax: (808) 974-4125

Cross-Reference/Focus: W, M, V, D, DV

University of Hawaii at Hilo - Career Center

Dr. Norman Stahl, Director
200 West Kawili St.
Hilo, HI 96720-4091
Telephone: (808) 974-7687
Fax: (808) 974-7689
Website: www6.uhh.Hawai'i..edu/careercenter

Cross-Reference/Focus: W, M,

Idaho

Boise State University - Women's Center/Cultural Center

Debby Woodall
1910 University Drive
Boise, Idaho 83725
Telephone: (208) 426-2407

Oregon

International Refugee Service Program

Debi Houghton / Miriam Ali
10301 NE Glisan
Portland, Oregon 97214
Telephone: (503) 234-1541

Job Corps Placement

Bob Williams
1130 SW Morrison, Suite 525
Springsdale, Oregon
Telephone: (503) 695-2245 ext. 252

Life & Career Options

Jackie Hubka / Betsey Rixford
19600 S Molalla Avenue
Oregon City, Oregon 97045
Telephone: (503) 657-6958 ext. 5161

Lives in Transition

Elaine Heck
1653 Jerome Avenue
Astoria, Oregon 97103
Telephone: (503) 338-2377

Employment Resource Referral Directory
Document Creation September 30, 2004
Document Last Revised –September 30, 2004
Cross-Reference Section: D=Disability; W=Women; M=Minority;
                        V=Veteran; DV=Disabled Veteran; PA=Public Assistance

Mid-Columbia Council of Governments

Bonnie Myatt
1215 Taylor Street
Hood River, Oregon 97031
Telephone: (541) 389-6300

Oregon Tradeswomen Network

Connie Ashbrook
1714 NE Alberta
Portland, Oregon 97211
Telephone: (503) 335-8200

Washington

YWCA - Seattle

1118 5th Ave
Seattle, WA 98101
Telephone: (206) 461-4888
Fax: (206) 461-4480
E-Mail: sfielder@ywcaworks.org

Cross-Reference / Focus: W

American Society of Women Accountants

Sharon O'Donnell, President
Dept 237, 800 5th Ave., Suite 101
Seattle, WA 98104
Telephone: (206) 467-8645

Cross-Reference / Focus: W

Association for Women Computing

P.O. BOX 179
Seattle, WA 98111
Telephone: (206) 781-7315

Cross-Reference / Focus: W

Womens Business Exchange

603 Stewart Street #610
Seattle, WA 98101
Telephone: (206) 284-2863

Cross-Reference/Focus:W

YWCA - Lynnwood

6027 208th Street S.W
Lynnwood, WA 98036
Telephone: (425) 774-9843

Cross-Reference/Focus:W

Women in Community Service

1111 3rd Ave Rm. 800
Seattle, WA 98101
Telephone: (206) 553-2082
Fax: (206) 553-6151

Cross-Reference / Focus: W

Washington Women's Employment & Education

1209 S. Central Ave Suite 105
Kent, WA 98032
Telephone: (253) 859-3718
Fax: (253) 859-1881
E-Mail: info@wwee.org

Cross-Reference / Focus: W

Washington Womens Employment & Education

Employment Resource Referral Directory
Document Creation September 30, 2004
Document Last Revised –September 30, 2004
Cross-Reference Section: *D=Disability; W=Women; M=Minority;*
                         V=Veteran; DV=Disabled Veteran; PA=Public Assistance

3516 S. 47th St., Suite 2405
Tacoma, WA 98405
Telephone: (253) 870-1624

Cross-Reference/Focus:W

Anew, Apprenticeship – Non-Traditional Employment for Women & Men

P.O. BOX 2490
Renton, WA 98056
Telephone: (425) 235-2212
Fax: (425) 235-7864

Cross-Reference / Focus: W

Society of Women Engineers

Angie O'Gorman, President
P.O. BOX 31910
Seattle, WA 98103
Telephone: (206) 622-4421

Cross-Reference / Focus:W

National Association of Women in Construction (Puget Sound)

Gwen Hart, President
P.O. BOX 97038
Redmond, WA 98073
Telephone: (425) 867-1234

Cross-Reference / Focus:W

C. Minority Services Listed by State

Alaska

NAACP

325 e. 3rd Ave
Anchorage, AK 99510
Telephone: (907) 272-8717

Cross-Reference/Focus:M

Tanana Chiefs

201 Fairbanks Ave
Fairbanks, AK 99701
Telephone: (907) 452-8251

Cross-Reference/Focus:M

Kodiak Area Native Association (KANA)

Kodiak, AK 99615
Telephone: (907) 486-5725

Cross-Reference/Focus:M

ONC Native Organization

P.O. BOX 927
Bethel, AK 99599
Telephone: (907) 543-2608

Cross-Reference/Focus:M

Metlakatla Indian Community

Merna Atkinson, Director
P.O. BOX 8
Metlakatla, AK 99926
Telephone: (907) 886-8376
Fax: (907) 886-4469

Employment Resource Referral Directory
Document Creation September 30, 2004
Document Last Revised –September 30, 2004
Cross-Reference Section: D=Disability; W=Women; M=Minority;
                    V=Veteran; DV=Disabled Veteran; PA=Public Assistance

Cross-Reference / Focus: M

California

Catholic Charities Diocese of Oakland

Barbara Terrazas, Executive Direcrtor
433 Jefferson Street
Oakland, CA 94607-3539
Telephone: (510) 768-3100
Fax: (510) 451-6998

Catholic Charities Diocese of Sacramento

Rev. Michael F. Kieman, Diocesan Director
2110 Broadway
Sacramento, CA 95818-2518
Telephone: (916) 733-0253
Fax: (916) 733-0224

Catholic Charities of the Archdiocese of San Francisco

Brain Cahill, Executive Direcrtor
2255 Hayes Street, Floor 4
San Francisco, CA 94117-1012
Telephone: (415) 592-9200
Fax: (415) 592-9201

Catholic Charities Diocese of San Jose

Diane Saign, Chief Executive Direcrtor
2625 Zanker Road, Suite 200
San Jose, CA 95134-2107
Telephone: (408) 468-0100
Fax: (408) 944-0275

Catholic Charities Diocese of Santa Rosa

Maureen E. Shaw, Executive Direcrtor
P.O. Box 4900
Santa Rosa, CA 95402-4900
Telephone: (707) 528-8712
Fax: (707) 575-4910

Catholic Charities Diocese of Stockton

James F. Rodgers, Executive Direcrtor
1106 N El Dorado Street
Stockton, CA 95202-1332
Telephone: (209) 948-1501
Fax: (209) 948-2559
Website: www.catholiccharitiesusa.org

Cross-Reference / Focus: M, W, V, DV

Employment & Career Services Center - Chabot College

Gerald Shimada, Interim Dean of Special Programs & Services
25555 Hesperian Boulevard
Room 2325, Building 2300
Hayward, CA 94545
Telephone: (510) 723-7228
Fax: (510) 723-7229
E-Mail: gshimada@chabotcollege.edu
Website:
www.chabotcollege.edu/studentservice/employcareer.html

Cross-Reference / Focus: M, W

Project Transition, Inc.

Joaquin Wallace, Executive Director
436 Fourteenth Street, Suite 100
Oakland, CA 94612
Telephone: (510) 808-0300
Fax: (510) 808-0305

Employment Resource Referral Directory
Document Creation September 30, 2004
Document Last Revised -September 30, 2004
Cross-Reference Section: D=Disability; W=Women; M=Minority;
                              V=Veteran; DV=Disabled Veteran; PA=Public Assistance

---

Website: www.project-transition.org

Cross-Reference / Focus: M, W, V, D, DV

Job Corps

Sacramento Job Corps Center

Ben Murti, Career Development Supervisor
3100 Meadowview Road
Sacramento, CA 95832
Telephone: (800) 698-3769 x2263

San Jose Job Corps Center

Richard Martinez, Community Director
3485 East Hills Drive
San Jose, CA 95127
Telephone: (408) 254-5627

Treasure Island Job Corps Center

Martina Proia, Community Director
655 H Avenue, Building 442
San Francisco, CA 94130
Telephone: (415) 277-2400 x2359
Website: http://jobcorps.doleta.gov

Cross-Reference / Focus: M, W

Alameda One-Stop

555 Atlantic Avenue
Alameda, CA 94501
Telephone: (510) 748-2208

Berkeley One-Stop

1950 Addison Street

Berkeley, CA 94704
Telephone: (510) 644-6085

Eastbay Works

120 Oak Street
Brentwood, CA 94513
Telephone: (925) 634-2195

Chico Employment Center

2445 Carmichael Drive
Chico, CA 95928
Telephone: (530) 895-4364

Clearlake Career Center

15880 Dam Road Extension
Clearlake, CA 95422
Telephone: (707) 995-7100

Colusa Career Resource Center

144 Market Street
Colusa, CA 95932
Telephone: (530) 458-0326

Eastbay Career Center

1875 Willow Pass Road
Concord, CA 94520
Telephone: (925) 646-5555

Mendocino Works Employment Resource Center

7600 Grange Street
Covelo, CA 95428
Telephone: (707) 983-0070

PAGE 33

Eastbay Works Tri-City One-Stop Career Center

39155 Liberty Street, Suite B200
Fremont, CA 94538
Telephone: (510) 794-3669

Eastbay Works Access Career Center

22225 Foothill Boulevard
Hayward, CA 94541
Telephone: (510) 888-7100

Lake Resource Center

341 N. Main Street
Lakeport, CA 95453
Telephone: (707) 263-0630

Employment Resource Center

6140 Horseshoe Bar Road
Loomis, CA 95650
Telephone: (916) 652-0933

California Indian Manpower Consortium

241 F Street
Eureka, CA 95501
Telephone: (707) 445-8451

Oakland East One-Stop

675 Hegenberger Road
Oakland, CA 94621
Telephone: (510) 563-5200

Oakland Career Center

1212 Broadway, Suite 100
Oakland, CA 94612
Telephone: (510) 768-4473

Red Bluff One-Stop Center

718 Main Street
Reb Bluff, CA 96080
Telephone: (530) 529-7000
Website: www.edd.ca.gov/one-stop

Cross-Reference / Focus: M, W, V, DV

Alameda County Private Industry Council

1212 Broadway, Suite 300
Oakland, CA 94612
Telephone: (510) 891-99393
Website: www.alcopic.com

Contra Costa County Private Industry Council

2425 Bisso Lane, Suite 100
Concord, CA 94520
Telephone: (925) 646-5382
Website: www.ccpic.org

Marin County Office of Employment & Training

2980A Kerner Boulevard, Room 2022
San Rafael, CA 94901
Telephone: (415) 499-6038
Website: www.citysearch.com/sfo/mec

Napa County Training & Employment Center

650 Imperial Way, Suite 109
Napa, CA 94558
Telephone: (707) 253-4339
Website: www.gotothehub.com

Employment Resource Referral Directory
Document Creation September 30, 2004
Document Last Revised –September 30, 2004
Cross-Reference Section: D=Disability; W=Women; M=Minority;
                              V=Veteran; DV=Disabled Veteran; PA=Public Assistance

San Mateo County Employment & Training Administration

262 Harbor Boulevard, Building A
Belmont, CA 94002
Telephone: (650) 802-5171

Solano County Private Industry Council

320 Campus Lane
Suisun, CA 94585
Telephone: (707) 864-3370
Website: www.edd.ca.gov

Cross-Reference / Focus: M, W, D, V, DV

Chinese for Affirmative Action

17 Walter U Lum Place
San Francisco, CA 94108
Telephone: (415) 274-6750

Chinese Center Employment Agency

128 Waverly Place
San Francisco, CA 94108
Telephone: (415) 362-4781

Cross-Reference / Focus: M, W

Filipinos for Affirmative Action

310 8th Street, Suite 308
Oakland, CA 94607
Telephone: (510) 465-9876

Cross-Reference / Focus: M, W

United Indian Nations, Inc.

1320 Webster Street
Oakland, CA 94612-3204
Telephone: (510) 763-3410

United Native Americans

2434 Faria Avenue
Pinole, CA 94564
Telephone: (510) 758-8160

Cross-Reference / Focus: M, W

The Unity Council (formerly Spanish Speaking Unity Council)

1900 Frutivale Avenue, Suite 2A
Oakland, CA 94601
Telephone: (510) 535-6900
Fax: (510) 534-7771
E-Mail: info@unitycouncil.org

Arriba Juntos

1850 Mission Street
San Francisco, CA 94103
Telephone: (415) 487-3240

Cross-Reference / Focus: M, W

Bay Area Urban League

303 Hegenberger Road, Suite A
Oakland, CA 94612
Telephone: (510) 548-6700
Fax: (510) 632-8291
E-Mail: baulinc@aol.com

Cross-Reference / Focus: M, W

Employment Resource Referral Directory
Document Creation September 30, 2004
Document Last Revised –September 30, 2004
Cross-Reference Section: *D=Disability; W=Women; M=Minority;*
V=Veteran; DV=Disabled Veteran; PA=Public Assistance

African Immigrant and Refugee Resource Center

4390 Telegraph Avenue, Suite E
Oakland, CA 94609
Telephone: (510) 547-6560
Fax: (510) 547-6559

Cross-Reference / Focus: M, W

Asians for Job Opportunities

1911 Addison Street
Berkeley, CA 94704
Telephone: (510) 548-6700

Cross-Reference / Focus: M, W

Glide Memorial Church

330 Ellis Street
San Francisco, CA 94102
Telephone: (415) 674-6175

Cross-Reference / Focus: M, W

Oakland Army Base Workforce Development Collaborative

John Brauer, Executive Director
2485 W. 14th Street
Oakland, CA 94607
Telephone: (510) 891-8773
Fax: (510) 891-8775

Cross-Reference / Focus: M, W

BACSIC

Zenobia Embry-Nimmer, Executive Director
2485 W. 14th Street
Oakland, CA 94607

Telephone: (510) 891-8773 x307

Cross-Reference / Focus: M, W

South of Market Employment Center

Judy Sorro, Executive Director
288 7th Street
San Francisco, CA 94103
Telephone: (415) 865-2105

Cross-Reference / Focus: M, W

Computer Training Consultants

144 San Tomas Aquino Road
Campbell, CA 95008
Contact: Kevin Easton, Vice President
Telephone: (408) 871-6636

Micro-Polytech Institute

1108 Walsh Avenue
Santa Clara, CA 95050
Contact: Alex Le, Director of Training
Telephone: (408) 492-9048

Institute for Business & Technology, Inc.

2550 Scott Boulevard
Santa Clara, CA 95050
Contact: Anne Batch Dougherty, Director of Placement
Telephone: (408) 727-1060, ext. 225

Central County Occupational Programs - Metropolitan Eduation District

760 Hillsdale Avenue
San Jose, CA 95136
Contact: Shirley Philipson, Career Center Manager

Employment Resource Referral Directory
Document Creation September 30, 2004
Document Last Revised –September 30, 2004
Cross-Reference Section: D=Disability; W=Women; M=Minority;
                          V=Veteran; DV=Disabled Veteran; PA=Public Assistance

Telephone: (408) 723-6416

Center for Training and Careers, Incorporated

1600 Las Plumas
San Jose, CA 95133
Contact: Job Developer
Telephone: (408) 251-3146
Telephone: (408) 251-3165
Website: www.ctcsj.org

One-Stop Career Center (EDD)

2450 South Bascom Avenue
Campbell, CA 95008
Contact: Pam Kenney or Nancy Kwan Employment
Representatives
Telephone: (408) 369-3606
Telephone: (408)-369-3680

Job Corps Center

3485 East Hills Drive
San Jose, CA 95127
Contact: Richard Martinez
Telephone: (408) 254-5627

Math, Engineering, Science Achievement (MESA) - San Jose State University Program

One Washington Square
San Jose, CA 95192-0080
Contact: Horacio Alfaro, Director
Telephone: (408) 924-3830

African American Community Services Agency

304 N 6th Street
San Jose, CA 95112
Contact: Adela Moreno, Office Manager

Telephone: (408) 292-3157
Fax: (408) 286-0619

Santa Clara University - School of Engineering – Minority Engineering Program

500 El Camino Real
Contact: Dee Peipho
Telephone: (408) 554-4468

Arbor Career Center

344 Salinas Street, Suite 202
Telephone: (831) 751-6002
Contact: Manuela Valdez, Brenda Sorrenson, Employment
Specialists

Arbor of Santa Cruz County

18 West Beach Street
Watsonville, CA 95076
Contact: Theresa Wright, Director
Telephone: (831) 763-8723

One-Stop Career Center (EDD)

2450 South Bascom Avenue
Campbell, CA 95008
Contact: Pam Kenney or Nancy Kwan, Employment
Representatives
Telephone: (408) 369-3606
Fax: (408) 369-3680

Workforce Connection - Employment Service Department

3022 N Blackstone, Suite 155
Fresno, CA 93726
Contact: Debbie Walter, Supervisor of Job Developers

Employment Resource Referral Directory
Document Creation September 30, 2004
Document Last Revised –September 30, 2004
Cross-Reference Section: D=Disability; W=Women; M=Minority;
                              V=Veteran; DV=Disabled Veteran; PA=Public Assistance

Telephone: (559) 230-4062 or 1-877-954-HIRE (to post jobs)
Fax: (559) 230-3600
Website: www.workforce-connection.org

Black Contractors Association, Inc. (BCA)

Abdur-Rahim Hameed, President
6125 Imperial Avenue
San Diego, CA 92114
Telephone: (619) 263-9791
Fax: (619) 263-6865
Website: www.bcasd.org

Cross-Reference/Focus: M

Neighborhood House Association

Gloria Jenkins
841 South 41st Street
San Diego, CA 92113
Telephone: (619) 263-7761
Fax (619) 263-6398

Cross-Reference/Focus: W, M

San Diego Urban League

Maurice Wilson, Director of Employment & Training
720 Gateway Center Drive
San Diego, CA 92102
Telephone: (619) 263-8196
FAX (619) 263-1938
Website: www.sdul.org

Cross-Reference/Focus: W, M, PA

Catholic Charities of Orange County

Xang Yang, Program Director, Employment Services
2323 West Lincoln Avenue, Suite 205
Anaheim, CA 92801

Telephone: (714) 635-5230
E-Mail: xangesa@ccoc.org
Website: www.ccoc.org

Cross-Reference / Focus: M

Center for Employment Training – Riverside Office

Pat Pendergraph, Director
9960 Indiana Avenue, Suite 9
Riverside, CA 92503
Telephone: (909) 351-3100
Fax: (909) 509-7655
E-Mail: patpxx@cet2000.org

Center for Employment Training – Santa Ana Office

Mary Hudge, Director
120 West 5th Street, Suite 120
Santa Ana, CA 92701
Telephone: (714) 568-1755
Fax: (714) 568-1331
Website: www.cet2000.org

Cross-Reference / Focus: M

Jobs and Employment Services Department (JESD) – San Bernardino JESD

646 North Sierra Way
San Bernardino, CA 92415
Telephone: (909) 386-0884

Jobs and Employment Services Department (JESD) – Colton Employment Center

851 South Mt. Vernon, Suite 7
Colton, CA 92324
Telephone: (909) 433-3400

Employment Resource Referral Directory
Document Creation September 30, 2004
Document Last Revised –September 30, 2004
Cross-Reference Section: *D=Disability; W=Women; M=Minority;*
V=Veteran; DV=Disabled Veteran; PA=Public Assistance

Website: www.sbcounty.gov/jesd

Cross-Reference / Focus: M, W, V, D, DV

Los Angeles Urban League/Pomona

264 East Monterey Avenue
Pomona, CA 91767
Telephone: (909) 623-9741
Website: www.laul.org

Cross-Reference / Focus: M, W, D

Mexican American Opportunity Foundation - Orange County

502 South Ross Street
Santa Ana, CA 92701
Telephone: (714) 835-4199
Website: www.maof.org

Cross-Reference / Focus: M

National Society of Hispanic MBAS - Orange County Chapter

Darwin Aguilar, Director of Human Resources
P.O. Box 01
358 S. Main Street
Orange, CA 92686
Telephone: (714) 505-1801
Fax: (714) 505-1802
E-Mail: hr@orangecounty.nshmba.org
Website: www.orangecounty.nshmba.org

Cross-Reference / Focus: M

National Tooling & Machining Assoc. (NTMA) - Training Centers of Southern California

Steve Albers, Administrative Director

13230 Firestone Blvd., Unit A
Santa Fe Springs, CA 90670
Telephone: (562) 404-4295

Cross-Reference / Focus: M, W, D, V, DV

Orange County/SER Jobs for Progress National, Inc.

Ronald Puente, Executive Director
1243 E. Warner Avenue
Santa Ana, CA 92705
Telephone: (714) 556-8741
Fax: (714) 556-0640
E-Mail: seroccal@aol.com
Website: www.ser-national.org

Cross-Reference / Focus: M

Regional Occupation Program (ROP) – Central County

Keri Gee Barnett, Community Relations Manager
2323 N. Broadway, Suite 301
Santa Ana, CA 92706
Telephone: (714) 541-5537

Regional Occupation Program (ROP) – Riverside County

PO Box 868
Riverside, CA 92502-0868
Telephone: (909) 826-6530

Regional Occupation Program (ROP) – San Bernardino County ROP

601 Noth East Street
San Bernardino, CA 92410-3093

Employment Resource Referral Directory
Document Creation September 30, 2004
Document Last Revised –September 30, 2004
Cross-Reference Section: D=Disability; W=Women; M=Minority;
                          V=Veteran; DV=Disabled Veteran; PA=Public Assistance

Telephone: (909) 386-2461

Cross-Reference / Focus: M, W, D

Southern California Indian Center – Fountain Valley Corporate Office

Frank Lucero, WIA Director
10175 Slater Avenue, Suite # 150
Fountain Valley, CA 92708
Telephone: (714) 962-6673
Fax: (714) 962-6343
E-Mail: scicgg@earthlink.net
Website: www.indiancenter.org

Cross-Reference / Focus: M

Hawaii

Hawaii - Island of Oahu

Alu Like, Inc.

Winona Whitman, Director of Employment/Training
458 Keawe St.
Honolulu, HI 96813
Telephone: (808) 535-6750
Fax: (808) 524-3744
Website: www.alulike.org

Cross-Reference/Focus: W, M

Associated Builders & Contractors, Inc. (ABC)

Dana Vennen, Director of Education/Training
207 Puuhale Rd., Ste. A
Honolulu, HI 96819
Telephone: (808) 845-4887
Fax: (808) 847-7876
Website: www.abc.org/Hawai'i

Cross-Reference/Focus: W, M

Catholic Charities Community & Immigrant Services

Dana Vennen, Director of Education/Training
712 N. School St.
Honolulu, HI 96817
Telephone: (808) 528-5233
Fax: (808) 531-1970

Cross-Reference/Focus: W, M

Department of Labor & Industrial Relations - Workforce Development Division

Suzanne Okazaki, Veterans Program Specialist
830 Punchbowl Street #329
Honolulu, HI 96813
Telephone: (808) 586-8881
Fax: (808) 586-8822
Website: www.dlir.state.hi.us\wdd

Cross-Reference/Focus: W, M, V, D, DV

Goodwill Industries of Hawaii, Inc

Mr. Dan Buron, Vice President of Human Services
2610 Kilihau Street
Honolulu, HI 96819
Telephone: (808) 836-0313
Fax: (808) 836-2579
E-Mail: dburon@higoodwill.org
Website: www.higoodwill.org

Cross-Reference/Focus: D, M, W, PA

Hawaii Hispanic Chamber of Commerce

Susana Ho, President

Employment Resource Referral Directory
Document Creation September 30, 2004
Document Last Revised –September 30, 2004
Cross-Reference Section: D=Disability; W=Women; M=Minority;
                               V=Veteran; DV=Disabled Veteran; PA=Public Assistance

P.O. Box 235263
Honolulu, HI 96823
Telephone: (808) 545-4344
Fax: (808) 550-8416

Cross-Reference/Focus: W, M

Hawaii Job Corp.

Lauree Nakata, Employment Transition Coordinator
49 S. Hotel St.
Empire Bldg. #205
Honolulu, HI 96813
Telephone: (808) 545-4344
Fax: (808) 550-8416

Cross-Reference/Focus: W, M

Hispanic Center of Hawaii

Nancy Ortiz, Executive Director
2044 S. Beretania St., Suite 2
Honolulu, HI 96826
Telephone: (808) 941-5216
Fax: (808) 941-1594
Website:
www.hometown.aol.com/latinladydjmv/centrohispano.html

Cross-Reference/Focus: W, M, D, V, DV

Honolulu Community College - Job Placement Office

Lorrie Cahill, Coordinator
720 N. King St.
Honolulu, HI 96817
Telephone: (808) 845-9207
Fax: (808) 847-9829
E-Mail: ulcahill@hcc.Hawai'i.ed
Website: www.hcc.Hawai'i.edu

Cross-Reference/Focus: W, M

Insights to Success, Inc

Ms. Mary Lou Clizbe, Executive Director
Ms. Myra L. Hager, Co-Executive Director
1154 Fort Street Mall, Suite 200
Honolulu, HI 96813
Telephone: (808) 532-8322
Toll free: (877) 532-8322
Fax: (808) 532-8324
E-Mail: its@alliedcom.net

Cross-Reference/Focus: D, M, W, V, DV, PA

JOINT EMPLOYMENT MANAGEMENT SYSTEM (JEMS)

Rita May, Director
Commander Navy Region Hawaii
1025 Quincy Ave., Suite 100
Pearl Harbor, HI 96860-4512
Telephone: (808) 473-0190
Fax: (808) 473-1402
Website: www.jemsHawai'i.com

Cross-Reference/Focus: W, M, V, DV

Kapiolani Community College - Job Placement Office

Carmen Simmons, Coordinator
4303 Diamond Head Rd., Manono 112
Honolulu, HI 96816
Telephone: (808) 734-9434
Fax: (808) 734-9877
E-Mail: ucarmens@Hawai'i.ed
Website: www.kccjobs.com

Cross-Reference/Focus: M

Kokua Mau Work Center

Ms. Yvonne Angut, Title

Employment Resource Referral Directory
Document Creation September 30, 2004
Document Last Revised –September 30, 2004
Cross-Reference Section: *D=Disability; W=Women; M=Minority;*
                    V=Veteran; DV=Disabled Veteran; PA=Public Assistance

2840 Waimano Home Road, Bldg. 9
Pearl City, HI 96782
Telephone: (808) 455-7847
Fax: (808) 455-8819

Cross-Reference/Focus: M, D

Leeward Community College - Office of Continuing Education and Training

Randall Francisco, Director
96-045 Ala Ike St.
Pearl City, HI 96782
Telephone: (808) 455-0477
Fax: (808) 453-6730
Website: www.lcc.Hawai'i.edu/ocet

Cross-Reference/Focus: W, M

National Association of Women in Construction

June Keaton, Past President
94-561 Kuaie Street
Mililani, HI 96789
Telephone: (808) 625-0441 or 833-4401
Fax: (808) 625-6604

Cross-Reference/Focus: W, M

Pacific Gateway Center (Formerly the Immigrant Center)

Dr. Tin Myaing Thein, Executive Director
720 N. King St.
Honolulu, HI 96817
Telephone: (808) 845-3918
Fax: (808) 842-1962
Website: www.pacificgateway.org

Cross-Reference/Focus: W, M

Samoan Service Providers Association (SSPA)

William Emmsley, Executive Director
2153 N. King Street #108
Honolulu, HI 96819
Telephone: (808) 842-0218
Fax: (808) 845-6539
E-Mail: sspa@sspa-hi.com
Website: www.samoanserviceproviders.com

Cross-Reference/Focus: W, M, V

YWCA OF OAHU

Sharon Gergurson-Quick, V.P. Managing Director
Human Resource Department
1040 Richards Street
Honolulu, HI 96813
Telephone: (808) 538-7061
Fax: (808) 521-8416
Website: www.ywcaoahu.org

Cross-Reference/Focus: W, M

Hawaii - Island of Kauai

Alu Like, Inc.

Remi Meints, Employment Training Coordinator
3100 Kuhio Hwy. C-6, C-7
Lihue, HI 96766
Telephone: (808) 245-8545
Fax: (808) 245-1720
Website: www.alulike.org

Cross-Reference/Focus: W, M,

Department of Labor & Industrial Relations - Workforce Development Division (Job Bank)

Tracy Hirano, Branch Manager

Employment Resource Referral Directory
Document Creation September 30, 2004
Document Last Revised –September 30, 2004
Cross-Reference Section: *D=Disability; W=Women; M=Minority;*
V=Veteran; DV=Disabled Veteran; PA=Public Assistance

3100 Kuhio Hwy. Ste C-9
Lihue, HI 96766
Telephone: (808) 274-3056
Fax: (808) 274-3059
Website: www.dlir.state.hi.us/wdd/lihue/

Cross-Reference/Focus: D, W, M, V

Kauai Community College

Nia Acob, Cooperative Education Coordinator
31-901 Kaumualii Hwy.
Lihue, HI 96766
Telephone: (808) 245-8328
Fax: (808) 245-8232

Cross-Reference/Focus: W, M

Kauai Economic Opportunity, Inc

Mabel Fujiuchi, Chief Executive Officer
P.O. Box 1027 (2804 Wehe Rd.)
Lihue, HI 96766
Telephone: (808) 245-4077
Fax: (808) 245-7476

Cross-Reference/Focus: W, M

Hawaii - Island of Maui

Alu Like, Inc.

Ms. Marlene Burgess, Employment Training Coordinator
1977 Kaohu Street
Wailuku, Maui, HI 96793
Telephone: (808) 249-9774
Fax: (808) 244-7880
E-Mail: mburgess@alulike.org
Website: www.alulike.org

Cross-Reference/Focus: W, M

Department of Labor and Industrial Relations – Workforce Development Division, Worksource Maui

Mr. Kevin Kimizuka, Acting Maui County Branch Manager
2064 Wells Street, #108
Wailuku, Maui, HI 96793
Telephone: (808) 984-2091
Fax: (808) 984-2090
Website: http://dlir.state.hi.us/wdd/

Cross-Reference/Focus: D, M, W, V, DV, PA

Maui Community College - Cooperative Education and Job Placement Services

Mr. Barry Takahashi, Job Placement and Retention Coordinator
310 Kaahumanu Avenue
Kahului, Maui, HI 96732
Telephone: (808) 984-3353
Fax: (808) 244-3228
E-Mail: uellenh@Hawai'i.ed
Website: http://mauicc.Hawai'i.edu\unit\coop\index.htm

Cross-Reference/Focus: M, W

Maui Economic Opportunity, Inc

Ms. Loretta Pacubas, Community Services Director
99 Mahalani Street
Wailuku, Maui, HI 96793
Telephone: (808) 249-2970
Fax: (808) 249-2971
E-mail: loretta.pacubas@meoinc.org
Website: www.meo.org

Cross-Reference/Focus: M, W, PA

Employment Resource Referral Directory
Document Creation September 30, 2004
Document Last Revised –September 30, 2004
Cross-Reference Section: D=Disability; W=Women; M=Minority;
                              V=Veteran; DV=Disabled Veteran; PA=Public Assistance

Hawaii - Island of Molokai

Alu Like Inc. – Molokai Island Center

Ms. Ruth Poaipuni, Employment Training Manager
P. O. Box 1859
Kaunakakai, Molokai, HI 96748
Telephone: (808) 553-5393
Fax: (808) 553-9998
E-Mail: rpoaipuni@alulike.org
Website: www.alulike.org

Cross-Reference/Focus: M, W, V, PA

Hawaii - Island of Hawaii

Department of Labor & Industrial Relations – Workforce Development Division (Job Bank)

Lori Sasaki, Kona Office Manager
74-5565 Luhia St., C-4
Kailua-Kona, HI 96740
Telephone: (808) 327-4770
Fax: (808) 327-4774
Website: www.dlir.state.hi.us/wdd/

Cross-Reference/Focus: D, W, M, V

Department of Labor & Industrial Relations - Workforce Development Division (Hilo Office)

Charlie Kunz, Hilo Office Manager
180 Kinoole St., Suite 205
Hilo, HI 96720
Telephone: (808) 974-4126
Fax: (808) 974-4125

Cross-Reference/Focus: W, M, V, D, DV

University of Hawaii at Hilo - Career Center

Dr. Norman Stahl, Director
200 West Kawili St.
Hilo, HI 96720-4091
Telephone: (808) 974-7687
Fax: (808) 974-7689
Website: www6.uhh.Hawai'i.edu/careercenter

Cross-Reference/Focus: W, M,

Idaho

Tero Director Nez Perce Tribe

P.O. BOX 365
Lapwai, ID 83540
Telephone: (208) 843-2253

Cross-Reference/Focus:M

Nez Perce Tribe

Richard D. Broncheau, Director
P.O. BOX 365
Lapwai, ID 83540
Telephone: (208) 843-7363
Fax: (208) 843-7365
E-Mail: rdbroncheau@nezperce.org

Cross-Reference / Focus: M

Kootenai Tribe

Pamela Rentz, Acting Director
P.O. BOX 1269
Booners Ferry, ID 83805
Telephone: (208) 765-2000
E-mail: prentz@teleport.com

Cross-Reference / Focus: M

Employment Resource Referral Directory
Document Creation September 30, 2004
Document Last Revised –September 30, 2004
Cross-Reference Section: D=Disability; W=Women; M=Minority;
      V=Veteran; DV=Disabled Veteran; PA=Public Assistance

Shoshone-Bannock Tribes

Denell Broncho, Director
P.O. BOX 306
Fort Hall, ID 83203
Telephone: (208) 478-3847
Fax: (208) 478-3756
E-Mail: dbroncho@shoshonebannocktribes.com

Cross-Reference / Focus: M

Coeur d'Alene Tribe

Marcia Stearns, Human Resource Director
P.O. BOX 408
Plummer, ID 83851
Telephone: (208) 686-5228
Fax: (208) 686-6216
E-Mail: mstearns@cddatribe.org

Cross-Reference / Focus: M

Oregon

Centro Latino Americano

Alberto Urquilla
944 W 5th Avenue
Eugene, Oregon 97402
Telephone: (541) 687-2667

Cow Creek Band of Umpqua Tribe of Indians

Martha Young-Foundation Administrator
2371 NE Stephens; Suite 100
Roseburg, Oregon 97470
Telephone: (541) 672-9405

El Programa Hispano

Juan Ocano
451 NW First Street
Gresham, Oregon 97030
Telephone: (503) 669-8350

Filipino American Association

Fred Austria
8917 SE Stark
Portland, Oregon 97216
Telephone: (503) 253-7636

Hispanic Access Center

Lupe McKee-Manager
1533 E Burnside
Portland, Oregon 97217
Telephone: (503) 236-9670

International Refugee Service Program

Debi Houghton / Miriam Ali
10301 NE Glisan
Portland, Oregon 97214
Telephone: (503) 234-1541

Job Corps Placement

Bob Williams
1130 SW Morrison, Suite 525
Springsdale, Oregon
Telephone: (503) 695-2245 ext. 252

Life & Career Options

Jackie Hubka / Betsey Rixford
19600 S Molalla Avenue
Oregon City, Oregon 97045

Employment Resource Referral Directory
Document Creation September 30, 2004
Document Last Revised –September 30, 2004
Cross-Reference Section: *D=Disability; W=Women; M=Minority;*
                    V=Veteran; DV=Disabled Veteran; PA=Public Assistance

Telephone: (503) 657-6958 ext. 5161

Lives in Transition

Elaine Heck
1653 Jerome Avenue
Astoria, Oregon 97103
Telephone: (503) 338-2377

Oregon Council for Hispanic Advancement

Greg Acuna
108 NW 9th, Suite 108
Portland, Oregon 97209
Telephone: (503) 228-4131 / (503) 241-9965

Hispanic Business Association

Alice Witney
10624 W Executive Dr.
Boise, Idaho 83713
Telephone: (208) 322-7033

Washington

Colville Confederated Tribes

Robert E. Louie, Director
P.O. BOX 150
Nespelem, WA 99155
Telephone: (509) 634-2716
Fax: (208) 634-2740

Cross-Reference / Focus: M

National Society of Black Engineers

3931 NE Brooklyn
Seattle, WA 98105

Telephone: (206) 543-4635

Cross-Reference / Focus:M

National Society of Hispanic Engineers

3931 NE Brooklyn
Seattle, WA 98105
Telephone: (206) 543-4635

Cross-Reference / Focus:M

United Indians of all Tribes Foundation

1945 Yale Place East
Seattle, WA 98102
Telephone: (206) 325-0070

Cross-Reference/Focus: M

Lower Elwha Klallum Tribe

Melvin J. Wheeler, Director
2851 Lower Elwha Road
Port Angeles, WA 98363
Telephone: (360) 452-8471
Fax: (360) 380-3428
E-Mail: mwheeler@elwha.nsn.us

Cross-Reference / Focus: M

Lummi Nation

Larry Priest, Director
2559 Lummi View Drive
Bellingham, WA 98226
Telephone: (360) 758-2799
Fax: (360) 758-9937
E-Mail: larryp@lummi-nation.bia.edu

Cross-Reference / Focus: M

Employment Resource Referral Directory
Document Creation September 30, 2004
Document Last Revised –September 30, 2004
Cross-Reference Section: *D=Disability; W=Women; M=Minority;*
                          V=Veteran; DV=Disabled Veteran; PA=Public Assistance

Bureau of Indian Affairs

Judy Joseph, Superintendent
2707 Colby
Everett, WA 98201
Telephone: (425) 258-2651

Cross-Reference / Focus:M

Commission on Asian American Affairs

Ryan Minato, Office Assistant
501 South Jackson
Seattle, WA 98104
Telephone: (206) 464-5820

Cross-Reference / Focus:M

Makah Tribe

Donna Scott, Director
P.O. BOX 115
Neah Bay, WA 98357
Telephone: (360) 645-3101
Fax: (360) 645-2127
E-Mail: dscott@makah.com

Cross-Reference / Focus: M

Muckleshoot Indian Tribe

39015 72nd Ave S.E
Auburn, WA 98092
Telephone: (253) 939-3311
Fax: (253) 939-5311

Cross-Reference / Focus: M

Western Washington Indian Employment Training Program

3701 6th Ave #344
Tacoma, WA 98406
Telephone: (253) 879-9066

Cross-Reference/Focus:M

Shoalwater Bay Tribal Council

P.O. BOX 130
Tokeland, WA 98590
Telephone: (360) 267-6766

Cross-Reference/Focus:M

Puyallup Tribe of Indians

Jesse Fisher, Director or Ronice Strickler, Acting Director
2002 E. 28th St.
Tacoma, WA 98404
Telephone: (253) 573-7905
E-Mail: Ronice@oz.net

Cross-Reference / Focus: M

Quinault Indian Nation

Lisa Sampson, Director
P.O. BOX 189
Taholah, WA 98587
Telephone: (360) 276-8211
Fax: (360) 276-4191

Cross-Reference / Focus: M

Spokane Tribe of Indians

Larry Brown, Director
P.O. BOX 99040
Wellpinit, WA 99040
Telephone: (509) 258-4581
Fax: (509) 258-9243

Employment Resource Referral Directory
Document Creation September 30, 2004
Document Last Revised –September 30, 2004
Cross-Reference Section: *D=Disability; W=Women; M=Minority;*
                              V=Veteran; DV=Disabled Veteran; PA=Public Assistance

Cross-Reference / Focus: M

Swinomish Tribe

Aurilia Bailey, Director
P.O. BOX 388
LaConner, WA 98257
Telephone: (360) 466-7232
Fax: (360) 466-3610

Cross-Reference / Focus: M

Tulalip Tribe

Teri Gobin, Manager
6103 31st Ave NE
Marysville, WA 98271
Telephone: (360) 651-3732
Fax: (360) 651-3474
E-Mail: gobin@tulaliptribes.net

Cross-Reference / Focus: M

Upper Skagit Indian Tribe

2284 Community Plaza
Sedro Woolley, WA 98284
Telephone: (360) 856-5501
Fax: (360) 856-6669

Cross-Reference / Focus: M

Black Student Division Office of Minority Affairs

1320 NE Campus Pkwy
Seattle, WA 98105
Telephone: (206) 685-0774

Cross-Reference/Focus:M

Yakama Nation

Randy Olney, Director
P.O. BOX 151
Toppenish, WA 98951
Telephone: (509) 865-5121
Fax (509) 865-6719
E-Mail: randyolney@aol.com

Cross-Reference / Focus: M

Suquamish Tribe

P.O. BOX 498
Suquamish, WA 98392
Telephone: (360) 394-5222

Cross-Reference/Focus:M

National Asian Pacific Center on Aging

1025 South King
Seattle, WA 98104
Telephone: (206) 322-5272

Cross-Reference/Focus:M

Tacoma Urban League

2550 South Yakima
Tacoma, WA 98405
Telephone: (253) 627-7964

Cross-Reference/Focus:M

Refugee Federation Service Center

7101 MKL South, Suite 214
Seattle, WA 98118
Telephone: (206) 725-9181

Employment Resource Referral Directory
Document Creation September 30, 2004
Document Last Revised –September 30, 2004
Cross-Reference Section: *D=Disability; W=Women; M=Minority;*
                                    V=Veteran; DV=Disabled Veteran; PA=Public Assistance

Cross-Reference/Focus:M

NAACP

105 14th Ave
Seattle, WA 98122
Telephone: (206) 324-6600

Cross-Reference/Focus:M

Central Area Motivation Program

Pat Russell
722 18th Ave
Seattle, WA 98122-4704
Telephone: (206) 812-4940
Fax: (206) 726-8483
E-Mail: Pat Russell 2001@qwest.net

Cross-Reference / Focus: M

Low-Income Minorities Center for Career Alternatives

901 S. Rainier Ave
Seattle, WA 98144
Telephone: (206) 322-9080

Cross-Reference/Focus:M

Urban League of Metropolitan Seattle

105 14th Ave
Seattle, WA 98122
Telephone: (206) 461-3792
Fax: (206) 461-8425
E-Mail: infor@urbanleague.org

Cross-Reference / Focus: M

Seattle Indian Center

611 12th Ave South, Suite 300
Seattle, WA 98144-2007
Telephone: (206) 329-8700
Fax: (206) 328-5983
E-Mail: sic@seanet.com

Cross-Reference / Focus: M

Commission on African American Affairs

1210 Eastside St. 1st Floor
Olympia, WA 98504
Telephone: (360) 753-0127

Cross-Reference/Focus:M

Japanese Community Service

1414 South Weller St.
Seattle, WA 98144
Telephone: (206) 323-0250

Cross-Reference / Focus: M

Eastside Multi-Ethnic Center

1811 156th Ave NE
Bellevue, WA 98007
Telephone: (425) 643-2221
Fax: (425) 644-8798

Cross-Reference / Focus: M

Black Dollar Task Force

116 21st Ave
Seattle, WA 98122
Telephone: (206) 323-0534

Employment Resource Referral Directory
Document Creation September 30, 2004
Document Last Revised –September 30, 2004
Cross-Reference Section: D=Disability; W=Women; M=Minority;
                    V=Veteran; DV=Disabled Veteran; PA=Public Assistance

Cross-Reference/Focus:M

Nooksack Indian Tribal Council

P.O. BOX 157
Deming, WA 98244
Telephone: (360) 592-5176

Cross-Reference/Focus:M

Centro de Ayuda Solidaria a los Amigos

220 Blanchard Street
Seattle, WA 98121
Telephone: (206) 956-0779

Cross-Reference/Focus: M

Sea-Mar Community Health Center & Social Services

8915 S. 14th Ave
Seattle, WA 98108
Telephone: (206) 764-0508

Cross-Reference/Focus: M

Central Latino Service

1208 South 10th Street
Tacoma, WA 98405
Telephone: (253) 572-7717

Cross-Reference/Focus:M

Concilio for the Spanish Speaking

115 N. 85th St. #200
Seattle, WA 98103
Telephone: (206) 706-7776

Fax: (206) 706-7773
E-Mail: concilio@NW.link.com

Cross-Reference / Focus: M

Indochinese Cultural and Service Center

1725 Drive East
Tacoma, WA 98408
Telephone: (253) 473-5666

Cross-Reference/Focus:M

Filipino Youth Activities

810 18th Ave
Seattle, WA 98122
Telephone: (206) 461-4870

Cross-Reference/Focus: M

Seattle Chinese Post

414 8th Ave South
Seattle, WA 98104
Telephone: (206) 223-0623

Cross-Reference/Focus:M

Chinese Information and Service Center

409 Maynard Ave South, Suite 203
Seattle, WA 98104
Telephone: (206) 624-5633
Fax: (206) 382-2089
E-Mail: info@cisc-seattle.org

Cross-Reference / Focus: M

Employment Resource Referral Directory
Document Creation September 30, 2004
Document Last Revised –September 30, 2004
Cross-Reference Section: D=Disability; W=Women; M=Minority;
                                V=Veteran; DV=Disabled Veteran; PA=Public Assistance

Korea Times

430 Yale Ave North
Seattle, WA 98109
Telephone: (206) 622-2229

Cross-Reference/Focus:M

Asian Counseling and Referral Service

720 8th Ave South, Suite 200
Seattle, WA 98104
Telephone: (206) 695-7600
Fax: (206) 695-7606

Cross-Reference / Focus: M

D. Disability Services Listed by State

Alaska

IAM Cares

650 International Airport Road, Suite 103
Anchorage, AK 99518
Telephone: (907) 562-3006

Cross-Reference/Focus:D

Division of Vocational Rehabilitation

1016 West 6th Ave., Suite 102
Anchorage, AK 99508
Telephone: (907) 274-9100

Cross-Reference/Focus:D

Division of Vocational Rehabilitation

3600 Bragaw
Anchorage, AK 99508
Telephone: (907) 561-4466

California

Goodwill Industries of Greater East Bay, Inc.

1301 30th Avenue
Oakland, CA 946601
Telephone: (510) 698-7200
Fax: (510) 534-0837
Website: www.eastbaygoodwill.org

Goodwill Industries of Sacramento Valley, Inc.

6648 Franklin Boulevard
Sacramento, CA 95823
Telephone: (916) 395-9000
Fax: (916) 395-2615
E-Mail: sacgw@pacbell.net
Website: www.goodwill.org/STATES/ca/sacremento.htm

Goodwill Industries of San Francisco, San Mateo, and Marin Counties Inc.

1500 Mission Street
San Francisco, CA 94103
Telephone: (415) 575-2100
Fax: (415) 575-2170
Website: www.sfgoodwill.org

Cross-Reference / Focus: D, DV

California Department of Rehabilitation – Chico District

Employment Resource Referral Directory
Document Creation September 30, 2004
Document Last Revised –September 30, 2004
Cross-Reference Section: *D=Disability; W=Women; M=Minority;*
V=Veteran; DV=Disabled Veteran; PA=Public Assistance

470 Rio Lindo Avenue, Suite 4
Chico, CA 95926-1899
Telephone: (530) 895-5507
TTY: (530) 345-3897

California Department of Rehabilitation – Mt. Diablo Delta District

1485 Enea Court, Suite 1100
Concord. CA 94520-5228
Telephone: (925) 602-3953
TTY: (925) 676-5623

California Department of Rehabilitation – Oakland District

1515 Clay Street, Suite 119
Oakland, CA 94612-1413
Telephone: (510) 622-2764
TTY: (510) 622-2796

California Department of Rehabilitation – San Francisco District

185 Berry Street, Lobby 7, Suite 180
San Francisco, CA 94107-1737
Telephone: (415) 904-7100
TTY: (415) 904-7138

California Department of Rehabilitation – Santa Rosa District

50 'D' Street, Suite 425
Santa Rosa, CA 95404-4764
Telephone: (707) 576-2233
TTY: (707) 542-6365
Website: www.dor.ca.gov

Cross-Reference / Focus: D, DV, M, W

Project Hired

1270 Franklin Mall
Santa Clara, CA 5050
Contact: Mila Wereta, Account Manager
Telephone/TDD (408) 557-0880
Fax (408) 557-0710
E-Mail: www.info@projecthired.org
Website: www.projecthired.org

Able-Disabled Advocacy (A-DA)

Elaine Cooluris, Director
2850 6th Avenue, Suite 311
San Diego, CA 92103
Telephone: (619) 231-5990
Fax (619) 231-2380

Cross-Reference/Focus: D

The Access Center

Val Vera, Employment Services Coordinator
1295 University Avenue, #10
San Diego, CA 92103
Telephone: (619) 293-3500
Fax (619) 293-3508

Cross-Reference/Focus: D

ARC of San Diego

John McKee, Director
9575 Aero Drive
San Diego, CA 92123
Telephone: (619) 571-0881
Fax (619) 571-1350

Cross-Reference/Focus: D

Employment Resource Referral Directory
Document Creation September 30, 2004
Document Last Revised –September 30, 2004
Cross-Reference Section: D=Disability; W=Women; M=Minority;
                                V=Veteran; DV=Disabled Veteran; PA=Public Assistance

Goodwill Industries of Orange County

Doug Wooley, Supportive Employment/NISH Supervisor
410 North Fairview
Santa Ana, CA 92703
Telephone: (714) 547-6301
Fax: (714) 541-6531
TTY: (714) 541-1873
E-Mail: Info@ocgoodwill.org
Website: www.ocgoodwill.org

Cross-Reference / Focus: D, DV

Hawaii

Hawaii - Island of Oahu

Department of Human Services - Division of Vocational Rehabilitation

Ms. Gwen Kagihara, Oahu Branch Administrator
600 Kapiolani Blvd., Room 301
Honolulu, HI 96813
Telephone: (808) 586-4828
Fax: (808) 586-5785
E-Mail: gkagihara@dhs.state.hi.us
Website: www.state.hi.us/dhs/vr.pdf
General inquiries should be e-mailed to Joy Patterson at:
jpatterson@dhs.state.hi.us

Cross-Reference/Focus: D

Department of Labor & Industrial Relations - Workforce Development Division (Honolulu Office)

Suzanne Okazaki, Veterans Program Specialist
830 Punchbowl Street #329
Honolulu, HI 96813
Telephone: (808) 586-8881
Fax: (808) 586-8822

Website: www.dlir.state.hi.us\wdd

Cross-Reference/Focus: W, M, V, D, DV

Goodwill Industries of Hawaii, Inc

Mr. Dan Buron, Vice President of Human Services
2610 Kilihau Street
Honolulu, HI 96819
Telephone: (808) 836-0313
Fax: (808) 836-2579
E-Mail: dburon@higoodwill.org
Website: www.higoodwill.org

Cross-Reference/Focus: D, M, W, PA

Hawaii Center for Independent Living

Ms. Pat Lockwood, Executive Director
414 Kuwili Street, #102
Honolulu, HI 96817
Telephone: (808) 522-5400
Fax: (808) 522-5427
TTY: (808) 536-3739
E-Mail: plockwood@DiverseAbilities.org
Website: www.hcil.org

Cross-Reference/Focus: D

Hispanic Center of Hawaii

Nancy Ortiz, Executive Director
2044 S. Beretania St., Suite 2
Honolulu, HI 96826
Telephone: (808) 941-5216
Fax: (808) 941-1594
Website:
www.hometown.aol.com/latinladydjmv/centrohispano.html

Cross-Reference/Focus: W, M, D, V, DV

Employment Resource Referral Directory
Document Creation September 30, 2004
Document Last Revised –September 30, 2004
Cross-Reference Section: D=Disability; W=Women; M=Minority;
                                V=Veteran; DV=Disabled Veteran; PA=Public Assistance

Insights to Success, Inc

Ms. Mary Lou Clizbe, Executive Director
Ms. Myra L. Hager, Co-Executive Director
1154 Fort Street Mall, Suite 200
Honolulu, HI 96813
Telephone: (808) 532-8322
Toll free: (877) 532-8322
Fax: (808) 532-8324
E-Mail: its@alliedcom.net

Cross-Reference/Focus: D, M, W, V, DV, PA

Kokua Mau Work Center

Ms. Yvonne Angut, Title
2840 Waimano Home Road, Bldg. 9
Pearl City, HI 96782
Telephone: (808) 455-7847
Fax: (808) 455-8819

Cross-Reference/Focus: M, D

Winners at Work

Ms. Sandy Kofel, Acting President
Ms. Rona Yagi, Acting Director of Program Services
414 Kuwili Street, #103
Honolulu, HI 96817
Telephone: (808) 532-2100
Fax: (808) 531-2108
E-Mail: info@winnersatwork.org
Website: www.winnersatwork.org

Cross-Reference/Focus: D, DV, PA

Hawaii - Island of Kauai

Department of Human Services - Division of Vocational Rehabilitation & Services for the Blind

Brenda Viado, Administrator
3060 Eiwa Street, Rm. 304
Lihue, Kauai, HI 96766-1877
Telephone: (808) 274-3333
Fax: (808) 274-3340

Cross-Reference/Focus: D

Department of Labor & Industrial Relations - Workforce Development Division (Job Bank)

Tracy Hirano, Branch Manager
3100 Kuhio Hwy. Ste C-9
Lihue, HI 96766
Telephone: (808) 274-3056
Fax: (808) 274-3059
Website: www.dlir.state.hi.us/wdd/lihue/

Cross-Reference/Focus: D, W, M, V

Hawaii - Island of Maui

Department of Human Services - Division of Vocational Rehabilitation & Services for the Blind

Paul Kiang, Administrator
54 S. High Street, Rm. 309
Wailuku, Maui, HI 96793
Telephone: (808) 984-8350
Fax: (808) 984-8355

Cross-Reference/Focus: D

Department of Labor and Industrial Relations – Workforce Development Division, Worksource Maui

Mr. Kevin Kimizuka, Acting Maui County Branch Manager
2064 Wells Street, #108
Wailuku, Maui, HI 96793
Telephone: (808) 984-2091

Employment Resource Referral Directory
Document Creation September 30, 2004
Document Last Revised –September 30, 2004
Cross-Reference Section: D=Disability; W=Women; M=Minority;
                                V=Veteran; DV=Disabled Veteran; PA=Public Assistance

Fax: (808) 984-2090
Website: http://dlir.state.hi.us/wdd/

Cross-Reference/Focus: D, M, W, V, DV, PA

Hawaii - Island of Molokai

Department of Human Services - Division of Vocational Rehabilitation & Services for the Blind

Jerome Mina, Rehabilitation Counselor
New State Office Bldg. Makaena Place
P. O. Box 1068
Kaunakakai, Molokai, HI 96748
Telephone: (808) 984-8350
Fax: (808) 984-8355

Cross-Reference/Focus: D

Department of Labor & Industrial Relations – Workforce Development Division – Worksource Molokai

Ms. Alberta Napoleon Lucas, Kaunakakai Local Office Manager
55 Makaena Place
Kaunakakai Civic Center, Phase II, Room 4
Kaunakakai, Molokai, HI 96748
Telephone: (808) 553-1755
Fax: (808) 553-1754
E-Mail: alucas@dlir.state.hi.us
Website: http://dlir.state.hi.us/wdd/

Cross-Reference/Focus: D, V, DV, PA

Hawaii - Island of Hawaii

Department of Human Services - Division of Vocational Rehabilitation & Services for the Blind

Cheryl Ann Takaba, Administrator
75 Aupuni Street #110
Hilo, Hawaii, HI 96720
Telephone: (808) 974-6444
Fax: (808) 974-6450

Cross-Reference/Focus: D

Department of Labor & Industrial Relations - Workforce Development Division (Job Bank)

Lori Sasaki, Kona Office Manager
74-5565 Luhia St., C-4
Kailua-Kona, HI 96740
Telephone: (808) 327-4770
Fax: (808) 327-4774
Website: www.dlir.state.hi.us/wdd/

Cross-Reference/Focus: D, W, M, V

Department of Labor & Industrial Relations – Workforce Development Division (Hilo Office)

Charlie Kunz, Hilo Office Manager
180 Kinoole St., Suite 205
Hilo, HI 96720
Telephone: (808) 974-4126
Fax: (808) 974-4125

Cross-Reference/Focus: W, M, V, D, DV

Oregon

Goodwill Industries of Oregon

Jim Worley
1943 SE 6th
Portland, Oregon 97214

Employment Resource Referral Directory
Document Creation September 30, 2004
Document Last Revised –September 30, 2004
Cross-Reference Section: D=Disability; W=Women; M=Minority;
     V=Veteran; DV=Disabled Veteran; PA=Public Assistance

Telephone: (503) 238-6176

Job Corps Placement

Bob Williams
1130 SW Morrison, Suite 525
Springsdale, Oregon
Telephone: (503) 695-2245 ext. 252

Life & Career Options

Jackie Hubka / Betsey Rixford
19600 S Molalla Avenue
Oregon City, Oregon 97045
Telephone: (503) 657-6958 ext. 5161

Lives in Transition

Elaine Heck
1653 Jerome Avenue
Astoria, Oregon 97103
Telephone: (503) 338-2377

Mid-Columbia Council of Governments

Bonnie Myatt
1215 Taylor Street
Hood River, Oregon 97031
Telephone: (541) 389-6300

Washington

Work Opportunities, Inc

6515 202nd St. SW
Lynnwood, WA 98036
Telephone: (877) 778-2555
Fax: (425) 670-1459
E-Mail: work-opportunities@worldnet.att.net

Cross-Reference / Focus: D

Lighthouse for the Blind

2501 South Plum
Seattle, WA 98144
Telephone: (206) 322-4200

Cross-Reference/Focus: D

Seattle Mental Health Institute

1600 E. Olive St.
Seattle, WA 98122
Telephone: (206) 324-2400

Cross-Reference/Focus: D

Washington Coalition of Citizens with disabilities (WCCD)

4649 Sunnyside Ave N., Suite 100
Seattle, WA 98103-6900
Telephone: (866) 545-7055
Fax: (206) 545-7059
E-Mail: lonnie@wccd.org

Cross-Reference / Focus: D

Seattle Diversity Works

14714 23rd Ave NE
Seattle, WA 98155
Telephone: (206) 364-9098
Fax: (206) 364-1214
E-Mail: info@seattlediversityworks.com

Cross-Reference / Focus: D

Employment Resource Referral Directory
Document Creation September 30, 2004
Document Last Revised –September 30, 2004
Cross-Reference Section: *D=Disability; W=Women; M=Minority;*
                    V=Veteran; DV=Disabled Veteran; PA=Public Assistance

Orion Industries

33926 9th Ave S.
Federal Way, WA 98003-6708
Telephone: (253) 661-7678
Fax: (253) 661-7843

Cross-Reference / Focus: D

Northwest Center

1600 W. Armory Way
Seattle, WA 98119
Telephone: (206) 285-9140
Fax: (206) 286-2300

Cross-Reference / Focus: D

Washington Council for the Blind

1503 Fifth Avenue W
Seattle, WA 98119
Telephone: (800) 255-1147

IAM CARES

9125 15th Place South
Seattle, WA 98108
Telephone: (800) 303-0426
Fax: (206) 764-0452
E-Mail: Inowack@IAM.CARESwa.org

Cross-Reference / Focus: D

Hearing, Speech & Deafness Center

1620 18th Ave
Seattle, WA 98122
Telephone: (206) 323-5770
Fax: (206) 328-6871
E-Mail: Job Developer: jws@hsdc.org

Cross-Reference / Focus: D

Goodwill Industries

714 South 27th St.
Tacoma, WA 98409
Telephone: (253) 272-5166
Fax: (253) 627-1248

Cross-Reference / Focus: D

Eastside Employment Services

1601 116th Ave NE Suite 102
Bellevue, WA 98004
Telephone: (425) 453-0676
Fax: (425) 453-0338
E-Mail: info@eside.org

Cross-Reference / Focus: D

Division of Vocational Rehabilitation, (DVR/DSHS)

1000 Central Ave South
Kent, WA 98032
Telephone: (800) 622-1375
Fax: (253) 395-5391

Cross-Reference / Focus: D

Division of Vocational Rehabilitation, (DVR/DSHS)

12063 15th Ave NE
Seattle, WA 98125
Telephone: (800) 622-1375
Fax: (206) 368-4608

Cross-Reference / Focus: D

Employment Resource Referral Directory
Document Creation September 30, 2004
Document Last Revised –September 30, 2004
Cross-Reference Section: D=Disability; W=Women; M=Minority;
                              V=Veteran; DV=Disabled Veteran; PA=Public Assistance

Division of Vocational Rehabilitation,
(DVR/DSHS)

14360 SE Eastgate Way
Bellevue, WA 98007-6462
Telephone: (800) 622-1375
Fax: (425) 649-4330

Cross-Reference / Focus: D

Division of Vocational Rehabilitation,
(DVR/DSHS)

18000 International Blvd Suite 1000
Seatac, WA 98188
Telephone: (206) 439-3703
Fax: (206) 439-3753

Cross-Reference / Focus: D

Diversified

13008 Beverly Park Rd.
Mukilteo, WA 98275
Telephone: (866) 884-3822
Fax: (425) 355-1261
E-Mail: ppowell@divind.com

Cross-Reference / Focus: D

AtWork

690 NW Juniper
Issaquah, WA 98027
Telephone: (425) 392-1812
Fax: (425) 392-1812
E-Mail: info@atwork-issaquah.com

Cross-Reference / Focus: D

Inland Empire Goodwill Industries

East 130th 3rd Ave
Spokane, WA 99202
Telephone: (509) 838-4246

E. Veteran's Services Listed by State

Alaska

Department Of Veteran Affairs

2925 deBarr Road
Anchorage, AK 99508
Telephone: (907) 257-4750

Cross-Reference/Focus:V

California

California Employment Development Department – Alameda County

675 Hegenberger Road
Oakland, CA
Telephone: (510) 563-5200

California Employment Development Department – Butte County

78 Table Mountain Boulevard
Oroville, CA
Telephone: (530) 538-7301

Employment Resource Referral Directory
Document Creation September 30, 2004
Document Last Revised –September 30, 2004
Cross-Reference Section: *D=Disability; W=Women; M=Minority;*
                          V=Veteran; DV=Disabled Veteran; PA=Public Assistance

California Employment Development Department – Calaveras County

571 Stanislaus Avenue
Angels Camp, CA

California Employment Development Department – Contra Costa County

330 – 25th Street
Richmond, CA
Telephone: (510) 970-7379

California Employment Development Department – Del Norte County

286 M. Street, Suite B
Crescent City, CA
Telephone: (707) 464-2112

California Employment Development Department – El Dorado County

4535 Missouri Flat Road, Suite 1A
Placerville, CA
Telephone: (530) 642-5516

California Employment Development Department – Humbolt County

409 K Street
Eureka, CA
Telephone: (707) 445-6532

California Employment Development Department – Inyo County

914 N. Main Street
Bishop, CA

Telephone: (760) 873-7185

California Employment Development Department – Lake County

15880 Dam Road Extension
Building 603
Clearlake, CA
Telephone: (707) 995-7100

California Employment Development Department – Lassen County

2545 Main Street
Susanville, CA
Telephone: (530) 257-6050

California Employment Development Department – Mendocino County

631 South Orchard Avenue
Ukiah, CA
Telephone: (707) 463-5710

California Employment Development Department – Marin County

3301 Kerner Boulevard
San Rafael, CA
Telephone: (415) 257-3625

California Employment Development Department – Napa County

650 Imperial Highway, Suite 101
Napa, CA
Telephone: (707) 253-9930

Employment Resource Referral Directory
Document Creation September 30, 2004
Document Last Revised –September 30, 2004
Cross-Reference Section: *D=Disability; W=Women; M=Minority;*
V=Veteran; DV=Disabled Veteran; PA=Public Assistance

U.S. Department of Labor
Employment Standards Administration
Office of Federal Contract Compliance Programs

California Employment Development Department
– Nevada County

10075 Levon Avenue, Suite 206
Truckee, CA
Telephone: (530) 582-7332

California Employment Development Department
– Placer County

1880 Sierra Gardens Drive, Suite 100
Roseville, CA
Telephone: (916) 774-4057

California Employment Development Department
– Sacramento County

2901 50th Street
Sacramento, CA
Telephone: (916) 227-0301

California Employment Development Department
– San Francisco County

801 Turk Street
San Francisco, CA
Telephone: (415) 749-7503

California Employment Development Department
– San Mateo County

271 92nd Street
Daly City, CA
Telephone: (650) 802-5000

California Employment Development Department
– Santa Clara County

2450 S. Bascom Avenue

Campbell, CA
Telephone: (408) 369-3606

California Employment Development Department
– Shasta County

1325 Pine Street
Redding, CA
Telephone: (530) 225-2088

California Employment Development Department
– Siskiyou County

310 Boles Street
Weed, CA
Telephone: (530) 938-3231

California Employment Development Department
– Solano County

125 Corporate Place
Vallejo, CA
Telephone: (707) 648-4024

California Employment Development Department
– Tehama County

718 Main Street
Red Bluff, CA
Telephone: (530) 529-7000

California Employment Development Department
– Trinity County

1248 Main Street
Weaverville, CA
Telephone: (530) 623-4893

Employment Resource Referral Directory
Document Creation September 30, 2004
Document Last Revised –September 30, 2004
Cross-Reference Section: *D=Disability; W=Women; M=Minority;*
                    V=Veteran; DV=Disabled Veteran; PA=Public Assistance

*California Employment Development Department
– Tuolumne County*

19890 Cedar Road, North, Suite B
Sonora, CA
Telephone: (209) 536-2971

*California Employment Development Department
– Yolo County*

25 North Cottonwood Street
Woodland, CA
Telephone: (530) 661-2601

*California Employment Development Department
– Yuba County*

1114 Yuba Street
Marysville, CA
Telephone: (530) 741-4218
Website: www.caljobs.ca.gov

Cross-Reference / Focus: V, D, W, M, DV

One-Stop Career Center (EDD)

2450 South Bascom Avenue
Campbell, CA 95008
Telephone: (408) 369-3606

Next Step Center

795 Willow Rd, MS 226B6
Menlo Park, CA 94025
Contact: Rose Sutton, Director
Telephone: (650) 617-2729
Fax (650) 617-2623
Website: www.nextstepjob.org (for posted resumes to
review)
Website: www.nextstep@nextstepjobs.org (post job
openings)

Veterans Industries

Jean Chadwick, VA San Diego Healthcare System
3350 La Jolla Village Drive
San Diego, CA 92161
Telephone: (858) 552-7532
Fax (858) 642-6312
Telephone: (800) 331-VETS (8387)
Website: www.va.gov/vetind/sandiego.htm

Cross-Reference/Focus: V, DV

*EDD, State of California - Veterans
Representatives - South Metro Career Center*

6145 Imperial Avenue
San Diego, CA 92114
Telephone: (619) 266-4274
Telephone: (619) 266-4239

Cross-Reference/Focus: V, DV

EDD, State of California

Joe Rodriguez, Veterans Representative
1550 West Main Street
El Centro, CA 92243-2888
Telephone: (760) 339-2716
Website: www.edd.ca.gov

Cross-Reference/Focus: V, DV

Center for Employment Training

Dora Mendivil, Director
3295 Market Street
San Diego, CA 92102
Telephone: (619) 233-6829
Fax (619) 233-1297

PAGE 61

Cross-Reference/Focus: W, M, V

Second Chance/STRIVE

POC: Scott Silverman
505 16th Street
San Diego, CA 92101
Telephone: (619) 239-1003
Fax (619) 239-1904 (Second Chance)
Telephone: (619) 234-8888
Fax (619) 234-7787 (STRIVE)
Website: www.secondchanceprogram.org

Cross-Reference/Focus: W, M, V, PA

San Diego Job Corps

Boyd Barger, Director
1325 Iris Avenue
Imperial Beach, CA 91932
Telephone: (619) 429-8500
Website: www.sandiegojobcorps.org

Cross-Reference/Focus: PA, M, W

California Employment Development Department – Anaheim

2450 E. Lincoln Avenue
Anaheim, CA 92806
Telephone: (714) 518-2323
Fax: (714) 518-2394

California Employment Development Department – Riverside

1151 Spruce Street
Riverside, CA 92507
Telephone: (909) 955-2200
Fax: (909) 955-2220

California Employment Development Department – Fontana

17590 Foothill Blvd.
Fontana, CA 92335
Telephone: (909) 350-8926
Fax: (909) 350-8942
Website: www.caljobs.ca.gov

Cross-Reference / Focus: V, D, W, M, DV

Villages at Cabrillo - VA Community Based Outpatient Clinic

Marvin DeBolt, Veterans Representative
2001 River Avenue
Building 28
Long Beach, CA 90806
Telephone: (562) 388-8000

Cross-Reference / Focus: V, DV

Hawaii

Hawaii - Island of Oahu

Department of Labor & Industrial Relations – Workforce Development Division (Honolulu Office)

Suzanne Okazaki, Veterans Program Specialist
830 Punchbowl Street #329
Honolulu, HI 96813
Telephone: (808) 586-8881
Fax: (808) 586-8822
Website: www.dlir.state.hi.us\wdd

Cross-Reference/Focus: W, M, V, D, DV

Employment Resource Referral Directory
Document Creation September 30, 2004
Document Last Revised –September 30, 2004
Cross-Reference Section: *D=Disability; W=Women; M=Minority;*
                                  V=Veteran; DV=Disabled Veteran; PA=Public Assistance

Hispanic Center of Hawaii

Nancy Ortiz, Executive Director
2044 S. Beretania St., Suite 2
Honolulu, HI 96826
Telephone: (808) 941-5216
Fax: (808) 941-1594
Website:
www.hometown.aol.com/latinladydjmv/centrohispano.html

Cross-Reference/Focus: W, M, D, V, DV

Insights to Success, Inc

Ms. Mary Lou Clizbe, Executive Director
Ms. Myra L. Hager, Co-Executive Director
1154 Fort Street Mall, Suite 200
Honolulu, HI 96813
Telephone: (808) 532-8322
Toll Free: (877) 532-8322
Fax: (808) 532-8324
E-Mail: its@alliedcom.net

Cross-Reference/Focus: D, M, W, V, DV, PA

JOINT EMPLOYMENT MANAGEMENT SYSTEM (JEMS)

Rita May, Director
Commander Navy Region Hawaii
1025 Quincy Ave., Suite 100
Pearl Harbor, HI 96860-4512
Telephone: (808) 473-0190
Fax: (808) 473-1402
Website: www.jemsHawai'i.com

Cross-Reference/Focus: W, M, V, DV

Samoan Service Providers Association (SSPA)

William Emmsley, Executive Director
2153 N. King Street #108

Honolulu, HI 96819
Telephone: (808) 842-0218
Fax: (808) 845-6539
E-Mail: sspa@sspa-hi.com
Website: www.samoanserviceproviders.com

Cross-Reference/Focus: W, M, V

U. S. Department of Veterans Affairs

Lionel Parker, Veterans' Service Officer
459 Patterson road #B-100
Honolulu, HI 96819
Telephone: (808) 433-0500
Fax: (808) 433-0381

Cross-Reference/Focus: V

Hawaii - Island of Kauai

Department of Labor & Industrial Relations - Veterans' Employment & Training Service

Eric Nordmeier, VETS Coordinator
3-3100 Kuhio Hwy., Suite C-9
Lihue, HI 96766
Telephone: (808) 274-3056
Fax: (808) 274-3059
Website: www.workwisekauai.com

Cross-Reference/Focus: W, M, V, D, DV

Department of Labor & Industrial Relations - Workforce Development Division (Job Bank)

Tracy Hirano, Branch Manager
3100 Kuhio Hwy. Ste C-9
Lihue, HI 96766
Telephone: (808) 274-3056
Fax: (808) 274-3059
Website: www.dlir.state.hi.us/wdd/lihue/

Employment Resource Referral Directory
Document Creation September 30, 2004
Document Last Revised –September 30, 2004
Cross-Reference Section: D=Disability; W=Women; M=Minority;
                                      V=Veteran; DV=Disabled Veteran; PA=Public Assistance

Cross-Reference/Focus: D, W, M, V

Hawaii - Island of Molokai

Alu Like Inc. - Molokai Island Center

Ms. Ruth Poaipuni, Employment Training Manager
P. O. Box 1859
Kaunakakai, Molokai, HI 96748
Telephone: (808) 553-5393
Fax: (808) 553-9998
E-Mail: rpoaipuni@alulike.org
Website: www.alulike.org

Cross-Reference/Focus: M, W, V, PA

Department of Labor & Industrial Relations – Workforce Development Division – Worksource Molokai

Ms. Alberta Napoleon Lucas, Kaunakakai Local Office Manager
55 Makaena Place
Kaunakakai Civic Center, Phase II, Room 4
Kaunakakai, Molokai, HI 96748
Telephone: (808) 553-1755
Fax: (808) 553-1754
E-Mail: alucas@dlir.state.hi.us
Website: http://dlir.state.hi.us/wdd/

Cross-Reference/Focus: D, V, DV, PA

Hawaii - Island of Hawaii

Department of Labor & Industrial Relations – Workforce Development Division (Hilo Office)

Charlie Kunz, Hilo Office Manager
180 Kinoole St., Suite 205

Hilo, HI 96720
Telephone: (808) 974-4126
Fax: (808) 974-4125

Cross-Reference/Focus: W, M, V, D, DV

Department of Labor & Industrial Relations - Workforce Development Division (Job Bank)

Lori Sasaki, Kona Office Manager
74-5565 Luhia St., C-4
Kailua-Kona, HI 96740
Telephone: (808) 327-4770
Fax: (808) 327-4774
Website: www.dlir.state.hi.us/wdd/

Cross-Reference/Focus: D, W, M, V

Oregon

Goodwill Industries of Oregon

Jim Worley
1943 SE 6th
Portland, Oregon 97214
Telephone: (503) 238-6176

International Refugee Service Program

Debi Houghton / Miriam Ali
10301 NE Glisan
Portland, Oregon 97214
Telephone: (503) 234-1541

Job Corps Placement

Bob Williams
1130 SW Morrison, Suite 525
Springsdale, Oregon
Telephone: (503) 695-2245 ext. 252

Employment Resource Referral Directory
Document Creation September 30, 2004
Document Last Revised –September 30, 2004
Cross-Reference Section: D=Disability; W=Women; M=Minority;
                           V=Veteran; DV=Disabled Veteran; PA=Public Assistance

Life & Career Options

Jackie Hubka / Betsey Rixford
19600 S Molalla Avenue
Oregon City, Oregon 97045
Telephone: (503) 657-6958 ext. 5161

Lives in Transition

Elaine Heck
1653 Jerome Avenue
Astoria, Oregon 97103
Telephone: (503) 338-2377

Mid-Columbia Council of Governments

Bonnie Myatt
1215 Taylor Street
Hood River, Oregon 97031
Telephone: (541) 389-6300

Washington

Veterans Independent Enterprises of WA

4630 16th St. East, Suite B-16
Fife, WA 98003
Telephone: (253) 922-5650

King County Veterans Office

123 3rd Ave South, Suite 300 Walthew Bldg.
Seattle, WA 98104
Telephone: (206) 296-7656

Veterans Readjustment Counseling Center

2030 9th Avenue South, suite 210
Seattle, WA 98121
Telephone: (206) 553-2706

Cross-Reference/Focus:V

Veterans Affairs Puget Sound Health Care

1660 South Columbia Way, M/S 117
Seattle, WA 98108
Telephone: (206) 762-1010 ext. 61982

Cross-Reference/Focus:V

Department of Veteran Affairs

Jackson Federal Building
915 Second Ave
Seattle, WA 98108
Telephone: (800) 827-1000

Cross-Reference/Focus:V

F. Disabled Veteran's Services Listed by State

Hawaii

Hawaii - Island of Oahu

Hispanic Center of Hawaii

Nancy Ortiz, Executive Director
2044 S. Beretania St., Suite 2

Employment Resource Referral Directory
Document Creation September 30, 2004
Document Last Revised –September 30, 2004
Cross-Reference Section: D=Disability; W=Women; M=Minority; V=Veteran; DV=Disabled Veteran; PA=Public Assistance

Honolulu, HI 96826
Telephone: (808) 941-5216
Fax: (808) 941-1594
Website:
www.hometown.aol.com/latinladydjmv/centrohispano.html

Cross-Reference/Focus: W, M, D, V, DV

Insights to Success, Inc

Ms. Mary Lou Clizbe, Executive Director
Ms. Myra L. Hager, Co-Executive Director
1154 Fort Street Mall, Suite 200
Honolulu, HI 96813
Telephone: (808) 532-8322
Toll Free: (877) 532-8322
Fax: (808) 532-8324
E-Mail: its@alliedcom.net

Cross-Reference/Focus: D, M, W, V, DV, PA

JOINT EMPLOYMENT MANAGEMENT SYSTEM (JEMS)

Rita May, Director
Commander Navy Region Hawaii
1025 Quincy Ave., Suite 100
Pearl Harbor, HI 96860-4512
Telephone: (808) 473-0190
Fax: (808) 473-1402
Website: www.jemsHawai'i.com

Cross-Reference/Focus: W, M, V, DV

U. S. Department of Veterans Affairs - Vocational Rehab Counseling Division

Edward Gavigan, Chief
459 Patterson Road #B-109
Honolulu, HI 96819
Telephone: (808) 433-0560
Fax: (808) 433-0382

Cross-Reference/Focus: DV

Winners at Work

Ms. Sandy Kofel, Acting President
Ms. Rona Yagi, Acting Director of Program Services
414 Kuwili Street, #103
Honolulu, HI 96817
Telephone: (808) 532-2100
Fax: (808) 531-2108
E-Mail: info@winnersatwork.org
Website: www.winnersatwork.org

Cross-Reference/Focus: D, DV, PA

Department of Labor & Industrial Relations – Workforce Development Division (Honolulu Office)

Suzanne Okazaki, Veterans Program Specialist
830 Punchbowl Street #329
Honolulu, HI 96813
Telephone: (808) 586-8881
Fax: (808) 586-8822
Website: www.dlir.state.hi.us\wdd

Cross-Reference/Focus: W, M, V, D, DV

Department of Labor & Industrial Relations – Workforce Development Division

Clyde Kawakami, Disabled Veterans Outreach Counselor
Vet Center- Outreach/Readjustment Counseling
1680 Kapiolani Blvd.
Honolulu, HI 96814
Telephone: (808) 973-8387
Fax: (808) 973-5295

Cross-Reference/Focus: DV, V

Employment Resource Referral Directory
Document Creation September 30, 2004
Document Last Revised –September 30, 2004
Cross-Reference Section: D=Disability; W=Women; M=Minority;
                                  V=Veteran; DV=Disabled Veteran; PA=Public Assistance

Hawaii - Island of Maui

Department of Labor and Industrial Relations – Workforce Development Division, Worksource Maui

Mr. Kevin Kimizuka, Acting Maui County Branch Manager
2064 Wells Street, #108
Wailuku, Maui, HI 96793
Telephone: (808) 984-2091
Fax: (808) 984-2090
Website: http://dlir.state.hi.us/wdd/

Cross-Reference/Focus: D, M, W, V, DV, PA

Hawaii - Island of Molokai

Department of Labor & Industrial Relations – Workforce Development Division – Worksource Molokai

Ms. Alberta Napoleon Lucas, Kaunakakai Local Office Manager
55 Makaena Place
Kaunakakai Civic Center, Phase II, Room 4
Kaunakakai, Molokai, HI 96748
Telephone: (808) 553-1755
Fax: (808) 553-1754
E-Mail: alucas@dlir.state.hi.us
Website: http://dlir.state.hi.us/wdd/

Cross-Reference/Focus: D, V, DV, PA

Hawaii - Island of Hawaii

Department of Labor & Industrial Relations – Workforce Development Division (Hilo Office)

Charlie Kunz, Hilo Office Manager

180 Kinoole St., Suite 205
Hilo, HI 96720
Telephone: (808) 974-4126
Fax: (808) 974-4125

Cross-Reference/Focus: W, M, V, D, DV

G. Public Assistance Services Listed by State

Hawaii

Hawaii - Island of Oahu

Goodwill Industries of Hawaii, Inc

Mr. Dan Buron, Vice President of Human Services
2610 Kilihau Street
Honolulu, HI 96819
Telephone: (808) 836-0313
Fax: (808) 836-2579
E-Mail: dburon@higoodwill.org
Website: www.higoodwill.org

Cross-Reference/Focus: D, M, W, PA

Insights to Success, Inc

Ms. Mary Lou Clizbe, Executive Director
Ms. Myra L. Hager, Co-Executive Director
1154 Fort Street Mall, Suite 200
Honolulu, HI 96813
Telephone: (808) 532-8322
Toll Free: 1-877-532-8322
Fax: (808) 532-8324
E-Mail: its@alliedcom.net

Cross-Reference/Focus: D, M, W, V, DV, PA

Employment Resource Referral Directory
Document Creation September 30, 2004
Document Last Revised –September 30, 2004
Cross-Reference Section: D=Disability; W=Women; M=Minority;
                    V=Veteran; DV=Disabled Veteran; PA=Public Assistance

Winners at Work

Ms. Sandy Kofel, Acting President
Ms. Rona Yagi, Acting Director of Program Services
414 Kuwili Street, #103
Honolulu, HI 96817
Telephone: (808) 532-2100
Fax: (808) 531-2108
E-Mail: info@winnersatwork.org
Website: www.winnersatwork.org

Cross-Reference/Focus: D, DV, PA

Hawaii - Island of Maui

*Department of Labor and Industrial Relations –
Workforce Development Division, Worksource
Maui*

Mr. Kevin Kimizuka, Acting Maui County Branch Manager
2064 Wells Street, #108
Wailuku, Maui, HI 96793
Telephone: (808) 984-2091
Fax: (808) 984-2090
Website: http://dlir.state.hi.us/wdd/

Cross-Reference/Focus: D, M, W, V, DV, PA

Maui Economic Opportunity, Inc

Ms. Loretta Pacubas, Community Services Director
99 Mahalani Street
Wailuku, Maui, HI 96793
Telephone: (808) 249-2970
Fax: (808) 249-2971
E-Mail: loretta.pacubas@meoinc.org
Website: www.meo.org

Cross-Reference/Focus: M, W, PA

Hawaii - Island of Molokai

Alu Like Inc. - Molokai Island Center

Ms. Ruth Poaipuni, Employment Training Manager
P. O. Box 1859
Kaunakakai, Molokai, HI 96748
Telephone: (808) 553-5393
Fax: (808) 553-9998
E-Mail: rpoaipuni@alulike.org
Website: www.alulike.org

Cross-Reference/Focus: M, W, V, PA

*Department of Labor & Industrial Relations –
Workforce Development Division – Worksource
Molokai*

Ms. Alberta Napoleon Lucas, Kaunakakai Local Office
Manager
55 Makaena Place
Kaunakakai Civic Center, Phase II, Room 4
Kaunakakai, Molokai, HI 96748
Telephone: (808) 553-1755
Fax: (808) 553-1754
E-Mail: alucas@dlir.state.hi.us
Website: http://dlir.state.hi.us/wdd/

Cross-Reference/Focus: D, V, DV, PA

H. Professional Association Services Listed by State

Alaska

Alaska Society of Professional Engineers

Employment Resource Referral Directory
Document Creation September 30, 2004
Document Last Revised –September 30, 2004
Cross-Reference Section: D=Disability; W=Women; M=Minority;
                              V=Veteran; DV=Disabled Veteran; PA=Public Assistance

Donald Dent, Executive Director
2064 Belair Drive
Anchorage, AK 99517
Telephone: (907) 277-6855
Fax: (907) 277-6855
E-Mail: drdeent@alaska.com

ABC – Associated Builders & Contractors

Ron Clemens, President
3680 C. Street., Suite 100
Anchorage, AK 99503
Telephone: (907) 565-5600
Fax: (907) 565-5645

Alaska Air Carriers Association

Bob Hajdukovich, President
929 E. 81st Ave
Anchorage, AK 99518
Telephone: (907) 277-0071
Fax: (907) 277-0072

Alaska Native Coalition on Employment and Training (ANCET)

Rachel Fisher, Administrator
1399 West 34th Ave, Suite 204
Anchorage, AK 99501
Telephone: (907) 644-8312
Fax: (907) 646-9287

Alaska Nurses Association

Camnille Soleil, Executive Director
2207 East Tudor Road, Suite 34
Anchorage, AK 99507
Telephone: (907) 274-0827
Fax: (907) 272-0292

Alaska Oil and Gas Association

Theresa Rockhill, Administrator
121 West Fireweed Lane, Suite 207
Anchorage, AK 99503
Telephone: (907) 272-1481
Fax: (907) 279-8114

Anchorage Home Builders Association, Inc

Vicki Portwood, Executive Director
8301 Schoon St., Suite 200
Anchorage, AK 99518
Telephone: (907) 522-3605
Fax: (907) 522-3754

Associated General Contractors of Alaska

Richard Cattanach, Executive Director
8005 Schoon St
Anchorage, AK 99518
Telephone: (907) 516-5354
Fax: (907) 562-6118

Mat-Su Home Builders Association

Emma Markley, Executive Director
165 East Parks Highway, Suite 206
Wasilla, AK 99654
Telephone: (907) 376-2666
Fax: (907) 376-2667

National Electrical Contractors Association – Alaska Chapter

Steve Boyd, Chapter Manager
712 West 36th Ave
Anchorage, AK 99503
Telephone: (907) 561-1958
Fax: (907) 561-8633

Employment Resource Referral Directory
Document Creation September 30, 2004
Document Last Revised –September 30, 2004
Cross-Reference Section: *D=Disability; W=Women; M=Minority;*
      V=Veteran; DV=Disabled Veteran; PA=Public Assistance

Washington

Greater Seattle Business Association

Luise Chernin, Executive Director
2150 N. 107th
Seattle, WA 98133
Telephone: (206) 363-9188

Tacoma-Pierce County Employment and Training Consortium

Kathryn Tyler, Administrative Assistant
3650 South Cedar
Tacoma, WA 98409
Telephone: (253) 591-5450

Washington Biotechnology and Biomedical Association

Ruth Scott, President
1100 Olive Way, Suite 300
Seattle, WA 98101
Telephone: (206) 624-1967
FAX: (206) 628-0899
E-Mail: washbio@washbio.org

Washington Society of Professional Engineers

Carrie Johnson, Executive Administrator
P.O. BOX 896
Olympia, WA 98507
Telephone: (360) 352-7437
Fax: (360) 586-5538
E-Mail: cjohnson@wabo.org

Employment Resource Referral Directory
Document Creation September 30, 2004
Document Last Revised –September 30, 2004
Cross-Reference Section: *D=Disability; W=Women; M=Minority;*
                              V=Veteran; DV=Disabled Veteran; PA=Public Assistance

Employment Resource Referral Directory
Document Creation September 30, 2004
Document Last Revised –September 30, 2004
Cross-Reference Section: *D=Disability; W=Women; M=Minority;*
                                    V=Veteran; DV=Disabled Veteran; PA=Public Assistance